GIRL NEXT DOOR

The Life and Career of

Jeanne Crain

Rupert Alistair

**Copyright © 2017
Rupert Alistair
All Rights Reserved**

All rights reserved. In accordance with the U.S. Copyright Act of 1976, the scanning, uploading, and electronic sharing of any part of this book without the permission of the publisher constitute unlawful piracy and theft of the author's intellectual property. If you would like to use material from the book (other than for review purposes), prior written permission must be obtained by contacting the publisher at permissions@hbgusa.com. Thank you for your support of the author's rights.

Table of Contents

{ 1 } Heartland Heritage, West Coast Dreams 5

{ 2 } Orson Welles and the Beauty Queen 20

{ 3 } Zanuck and His Rising Star 34

{ 4 } Twentieth Century-Fox Presents "The Girl Next Door" 49

{ 5 } Paul 60

{ 6 } 1946 – The Year of Jeanne 72

{ 7 } Motherhood and Addie Ross 83

{ 8 } Pinky 97

{ 9 } Teen Angst at 25 107

{ 10 } Goodbye, Fox 119

{ 11 } Divorce Court 137

{ 12 } A New Beginning 152

{ 13 } The Family Brinkman (and Crain) 171

{ 14 } An Armful of Babies or a Scrapbook Full of Screen Credits 185

A Note to Loyal Readers and Classic Movie Fans 203

ACKNOWLEDGEMENTS 204

NOTES AND REFERENCES 206

BIBLIOGRAPHY 237

{ 1 }
Heartland Heritage, West Coast Dreams

To a crowd of 50,000 onlookers, Grauman's Chinese Theater opened its elaborate doors in May 1927. The occasion was celebrated by the premiere of director Cecil B. DeMille's silent Biblical epic, *The King of Kings*. For decades to come, and a few name changes, Grauman's Chinese was a place of glamour and opulence, showcasing Hollywood's biggest movies and its brightest stars. But the films that played within its pagoda-like façade were secondary to its real claim to fame. The public flocked to the iconic Hollywood Boulevard landmark to see the hand and feet imprints of their favorite Tinsel Town stars, formed for posterity in the sidewalk cement. The theater courtyard boasted not only Clark Gable's handprints, but also the impression of Betty Grable's famous legs, and John Barrymore's infamous profile.

On a pleasant October evening in 1949, Twentieth Century-Fox star, Jeanne Crain, joined the exclusive ranks of Barbara Stanwyck and Humphrey Bogart, with her own space in the celebrated promenade. There, beside a spot that would eventually be immortalized by Cary Grant in 1951, the actress personalized a message for the theater's representative, Sid Grauman, in her own, very feminine handwriting: *To Sid, My Greatest Thrill*. Her first-born child, two-year old Paul Jr., was by her side, making for a cute, family-friendly photo opportunity which only enhanced Crain's wholesome, girl-next-door image. If a spot at Grauman's was an indicator of Hollywood success, Jeanne Crain was at the top of her game in late 1949, receiving her coveted niche in the cement two years prior to movie megastar Grant, and months before both John Wayne and Bette Davis. It was a high point in the Cinderella career of the comely actress, whose photogenic face and petite figure had graced over a dozen films since her debut in 1943. Unlike many in the movie land hierarchy, who clawed their way to stardom and struggled for years playing thankless parts, Crain's success came relatively quickly. The superstar status of Joan Crawford or Lana Turner may have eluded her, but, she nonetheless secured her place in mid-century Hollywood just as surely as she secured her spot at Grauman's Chinese.

Although she traveled abroad several times throughout her adulthood, both for personal pleasure as well as professionally to make motion pictures, Jeanne Crain was a quintessential California girl. She was born and raised there, worked as a mainstay in the Hollywood studio system for three decades, and lived out her last years in picturesque Santa Barbara. Her roots, however, were planted in the American Midwest, in areas as rural and homespun as the early characters she portrayed on film.

Jeanne Crain in 1949
(Courtesy of the Jeanne Crain Brinkman Family Trust)

****

George Adolphus Crain was born in the tiny hamlet of Sweet Springs, in western Missouri, in 1900. Shortly after his birth, his father, James, or Jim as he was known, moved the family to the prairie land of Egg Creek Township in rural McHenry County, North Dakota. The level plains of the area's farmland yielded many small lakes and had, in the not distant past, been the hunting grounds of various Indian tribes. Jim Crain became one of the burgeoning community's first leaders and one of its most prominent farmers, clearing $5,000 a year between 1902 and 1907, a very substantial amount of money at the turn of the twentieth century. Prosperity abounded in the region, and by the summer of 1921, Crain had "320 acres of corn knee high and looking fine." Education took an important position in his household, and the local school was situated on the southern portion of the Crain acreage. Jim's two older children, Luella and Leeper, would go on to college and post-graduate success as respected teachers.

When he graduated from nearby Granville High School in 1916, younger son George made his way to the University of North Dakota in Grand Forks. Intelligent and studious, he became very active in the arts community, auditioning for the University Men's Glee Club and getting his poetry published in the school's literary anthology. He became involved with the University's theater group, known as the Dakota Playmakers, where his interest in drama extended not only to acting and directing, but in playwriting as well. To encourage and support UND students who excelled in dramatic composition, Dr. J. G. Arneberg, an eye, ear, nose and throat specialist who practiced in Grand Forks, offered annual monetary awards to those students whose original play was written as classwork, then presented by the Dakota Playmakers.

The Arneberg Prizes were divided into two tiers, first prize being fifteen dollars and the second set at ten dollars. In 1920, George, then a junior, won the top Arneberg Prize for his one-act play, *Kara*, about a "beautiful Armenian dancer who finally, thru the good agencies of an American, escapes the clutches of Amil Bey and his Turkish harem." The idea for the story came when young Crain read a newspaper headline about two thousand Armenian refugees during the First World War who reached safety during an American mission. He imagined one of his characters among this throng and developed the play from there. *Kara*, along with two other Arneberg winners, was presented at the Metropolitan Opera House in Grand Forks in the summer of 1920 with George playing one of the roles.

His scholarly ambitions, however, weren't solely in amateur theatrics. In September 1918, the University of North Dakota welcomed two young Frenchwomen to their student body who studied on campus for several semesters. The experience was a positive one for all involved and the university felt that others might benefit from an expansion of the program. A similar interchange between UND and educational facilities in South America was investigated, resulting in negotiations with the University of Buenos Aires. A exchange plan between the two schools was approved in 1920 and upon his graduation from the Department of Education in 1921, George was announced as one of the first two UND representatives to go south of the border. Crain spent much of the autumn in New York City, visiting with a former member of the Dakota Playmakers, Ruth Baughman (who was trying her hand as a chorus girl in the big city), and preparing for his South American departure scheduled the following month.

After the New Year, Crain, along with fellow exchange student, Ernest Hurd, sailed for Panama, where they would remain until their school term in Buenos Aires began in March. Reports of their travels were relayed back to North Dakota by both participants, and George found the country very appealing, after getting accustomed to the newness of the situation as well as the language barrier. In October 1922, Crain wrote of expanding his geographical horizons even further: "Mr. Hurd and I think that we will go out into the country and try estancia [rural, ranch-style] life for a month or so. So far, we know nothing of the country except by hearsay. All our associations and information are with and concerning Buenos Aires."

After completing his South American experience, George returned to UND to finish up his post-graduate studies and receive his teaching certificate, and in 1923, he accepted the position of principal at the newly built Ray High School. Ray was a rural burg of five hundred residents in the northwest corner of North Dakota. It was a young community, just two decades in existence when George Crain took on the job as principal of the small local school.

Among the town's citizenry was Martin Carr, who had moved from Iowa in the early years of the century. Born in County Mayo, Ireland, Carr was a grocery merchant whose large family included middle daughter Loretta. Like the Crain family, the Carrs held education in high esteem, and Loretta followed in her elder sister Marie's footsteps by training to be a schoolteacher. After graduating from Ray High in June 1919, sixteen-year-old Loretta enrolled in the teaching program at the State Normal School in Valley City, North Dakota, a state sponsored facility "for the purpose of training teachers for the elementary schools, both rural and urban." During his time at the Ray school, George met and courted Loretta Carr. The couple married on June 12, 1924, and with opportunities for advancement in the small community scarce, the newlyweds headed west, where George took a teaching job in Barstow, California.

In the early twentieth century, Barstow was a busy and thriving rail center along the Santa Fe line, which heralded one of the famed Fred Harvey Houses, a site of hospitality for weary train travelers. Before the advent of the interstate highway system, the small mining town in the Mojave Desert was an important stop on both Routes 66 and 91. The two thoroughfares met in downtown Barstow and continued together to Los Angeles, which was ninety-five miles to the southwest. While living there, Loretta became pregnant, and on Monday, May 25, 1925, she gave birth to a daughter, Jeanne Elizabeth Crain. Nineteen months later on January 17, 1927, another little girl, Rita Marie, would follow. Loretta always wanted twins and having two blond-haired babies allowed her the luxury of dressing her daughters alike, leading people to believe they were indeed twins. The siblings were close from the beginning, and when Jeanne was told in the winter of 1927, "we have a baby sister for you," she literally wanted what was "hers."

Before Rita was born, George moved the family from rural Barstow to the Los Angeles suburb of Inglewood, where he had taken a position in the English department at Inglewood Union High School. Between 1920 and 1925, Inglewood, only eleven miles from downtown LA, was the fastest growing city in the United States with neat, tidy little bungalows being constructed at a rapid pace. The Crains lived in one of these small, newly built homes on Buckthorne Street, and by the summer of 1928, Loretta discovered she was expecting another child. Unlike her two previous pregnancies, this one did not result in a happy addition to their growing family. In the early evening on November 21, the week before Thanksgiving, a baby girl was stillborn at Inglewood's Centinela Hospital. The tragedy was compounded when Jeanne, then three and a half years-old, almost died after developing double pneumonia and empyema. She remained hospitalized for four months and returned home weighing only twenty-eight pounds. During her convalescence, her beloved Aunt Elizabeth, Loretta's youngest sister, taught Jeanne to read.

The Carr family had also moved from the Dakotas to the warm climate of Los Angeles in the mid- '20s and Mr. Carr would use his experience as a grocer to obtain work at a small store just a couple of blocks from their white stucco home on Van Ness Avenue. During their childhood, Jeanne and Rita would imitate their mother by calling their grandmother, "Ma", while addressing Loretta as "Mother." The Carrs would continue to play a role in their daughter's and granddaughters' lives. This support was extended even more in April 1932, when Loretta left George, after almost eight years of marriage.

Loretta Carr Crain, with her daughters,
Jeanne and Rita, 1930
(Courtesy of the Jeanne Crain Brinkman Family Trust)

According to her complaint filed in a Los Angeles divorce court, Loretta claimed that her husband had become "domineering, arrogant and brutal" toward her, even being "rude, impatient and irritable" on numerous occasions when they were with friends. He began staying out until the early hours of the morning and when Loretta asked where he had been he replied that "it was none of her damned business." He went on to tell his wife that she "would do exactly as he dictated and not otherwise," and that she would follow the "rules as he would lay down." Harsh words weren't the only things hurled at her. Physical abuse dated back several years, even during her pregnancy with her youngest child, when he kicked her out of bed, hit and threw furniture at her. The problem only accelerated in the months leading up to the divorce. In late November of 1931, he threw hot water at Loretta's face and a few weeks later he "choked, beat, hit and scratched" her, this time in the presence of Jeanne and Rita, who were six and four, respectively.

According to the complaint, the abuse continued after the New Year, when George again "beat and bruised" his wife, again in front of their daughters. By spring, she had had enough. On April 13, after being dragged by her husband out of bed and beaten for the second day in a row, she walked out, taking Jeanne and Rita with her. They moved into a six-room stucco bungalow on the same street as her parents, and Loretta went to see William Rains, a downtown Los Angeles divorce attorney. She sought custody of the girls and $150 per month in support from George's monthly teaching salary of $319. The twenty-nine-year-old mother hadn't worked outside the home since her days as a young teacher in North Dakota. To support herself and her children, she planned to attend nearby UCLA to acquire her teaching certificate, as her accreditation hadn't transferred to California.

The Carrs: (l-r), Mae Carr (Loretta's sister-in-law), Loretta, Rita, Anna Carr, Jeanne, and Martin Carr, mid-1930s
(Courtesy of the Jeanne Crain Brinkman Family Trust)

An interlocutory divorce was granted in June 1932, with custody going to Loretta, and allowing visitation rights to George, who was neither present nor represented during the hearing. For support, Mr. Crain was to pay $125 monthly, with the exception of $75 for the months of July, August and September, an offset to account for the school system's summer break. By January he was delinquent by $180 of the accrued amount and Loretta was back in court, this time with George present for contempt proceedings. In February, the court dismissed the case without prejudice and the final decree wouldn't be filed for thirteen more years, and then at the request of George Crain.

A return to teaching by Mrs. Crain didn't come to pass. Loretta was, however, a good seamstress, and to make ends meet she took in sewing, as well as working retail jobs. Jeanne and Rita watched their mother work herself to near collapse during these tough times, when sustenance often consisted of saltine crackers and cans of tomato soup. Even when Jeanne became a financially successful adult, she would sometimes partake of stewed tomatoes and corned beef hash, the comfort foods that had brought physical solace during her youth. When they could, the trio Crain loved to go to the movies, and they would often take in the less expensive afternoon matinees. One Christmas Day during the Depression, when Loretta was utterly exhausted from work, they went to see Astaire and Rogers in *The Gay Divorcee*. Their mother was so tired that she fell asleep during the showing, and Jeanne and Rita got to watch the picture three times.

George continued to play a part in his daughters' lives and their education. Born and raised Irish-Catholic, the Crain girls attended St. Mary's Academy, a private school located at Clauson Avenue and Crenshaw Boulevard in Los Angeles, where they were instructed by the Sisters of St. Joseph of Carondelet. Jeanne was dreamy and withdrawn and had "her nose forever in a book." She would later recall, "I was a quiet, introspective child. I lived in my imagination and my dreams and my books." With her favorite novel of those early childhood days being *Tom Sawyer*, she would imagine herself as Becky Thatcher and "Tom and Huck were more real to her than the children on the block." Her little sister, on the other hand, was outgoing and boisterous, "always ready to wrestle with the world on its own terms," yet accident prone, once breaking both arms at the same time.

Rita would often be sick and need attention for a health issue or accident consistently. Jeanne wasn't without her ailments, having scarlet fever, which required an eight-month quarantine of the Crain household. Protective of her older sister, Rita would lovingly tease her about reading in her own quiet world, but woe unto anyone else who tried it.

While still in grammar school, Jeanne discovered she had an aptitude for drawing and developed a keen interest in art. She hoped to pursue it as a career and enjoyed immensely her art classes at St. Mary's, painting "lovely Madonnas in oils," and reading about the lives of the old Renaissance masters. Then, while in the eighth grade, Jeanne was encouraged by Sister Mary Miles to audition for the class play. The kind and caring nun understood the young girl's painful shyness and realized that she wasn't aloof, only scared. Young Jeanne ended up winning the lead role in the play called *Scarface*, about a disfigured Indian maiden, and her interest in drama and acting blossomed. Her shy nature was overshadowed by the desire to use her creative spirit. "I came out of my shell in school plays when I could be somebody else but Jeanne Crain," she said.

As happy as she was at St. Mary's, it was around this time that she faced a teenaged dilemma. Since she and Rita were small, it had been the wish of their father for them to attend Inglewood High, where he continued a successful career in the English and Foreign language department. Jeanne had spent her childhood at St. Mary's, developing friendships with both her fellow classmates as well as the sisters who taught her, and she didn't relish the idea of transferring to a large school like Inglewood, "with 2,500 students and half of them *boys!*" Loretta was torn between wanting the girls to be

Rita, George and Jeanne
(Courtesy of the Jeanne Crain Brinkman Family Trust)

happy, and continue on at the Catholic school while still being fair to George. Also in question were the fees at the private institution. Jeanne's time at St. Mary's made a lasting impression on her. She would remain a devout Catholic her entire life, and even considered becoming a nun at one point, though her mother strongly dissuaded her from that direction.

It was finally decided that the Crain girls would join their father at Inglewood High, which meant, among other things, that the 1939-1940 school year would see them wearing colorful sweaters, skirts and bobbysocks instead of their familiar Catholic school uniforms. Jeanne began to make friends and meet boys. At St. Mary's, social activities with the opposite sex had been strictly monitored. The first dance the girls attended was the Loyola Junior Prom. Loyola was a Jesuit prep facility for boys and the oldest high school in southern California. If the girls at St. Mary's didn't have a date, the sisters would arrange for one, and a "charm expert" would come and give insight to make-up and clothes. Dresses for the occasion had to be deemed appropriate, with necklines high enough and sleeves low enough. Being schooled with only girls her whole life and having no brothers, boys were new to Jeanne. Before long, she would, however, attract them like bees to honey. Her photo in the 1940 Inglewood yearbook is that of a lovely teenager in a pensive pose. Inglewood High would offer her memories and opportunities that would carry over into a new and exciting future.

{ 2 }
Orson Welles and the Beauty Queen

By 1939, Loretta was working full-time as an office stenographer making $832 a year. In autumn of that year, Jeanne was getting settled in at Inglewood High School. Mrs. Carr helped her daughter with her role as a single parent and the Crain girls enjoyed a close bond with their maternal relatives (Loretta's youngest sister, Elizabeth, who had also become a school teacher, was still living next door with her parents). Jeanne was maturing into a beautiful girl. That was undisputable. She continued to pursue her interest in drama by entering and winning a prize at the annual Shakespearean contest hosted by Occidental College. Her personal confidence had increased to the point that in the summer of 1941, at the age of sixteen, she competed in the Miss California beauty contest as Miss Long Beach.

Jeanne and seventeen other girls from across the state came together on Friday night, July 25, in the hopes they might win a free trip to Atlantic City the following September, where they would represent California in the Miss America pageant. The event was sponsored by the American Legion and held at the Los Angeles Memorial Coliseum, where the Legion's color guard and musical organizations opened with all the pomp and pageantry expected of them. Popular crooner of a generation past, Rudy Vallee, was the presiding judge of a panel that included

Jeanne (seated center) as one of the beauty contestants
in the Miss Long Beach competition
(Courtesy of the Jeanne Crain Brinkman Family Trust)

the fashion editor of the *Los Angeles Times*, general editor of the movie magazine, *Screen Guide*, a talent scout and a cameraman from Universal Studio.

There, in front of a crowd of 3,000 spectators, the young beauties paraded across the west end of the stadium first in bathing suits, then in evening gowns. As the festivities of the evening wound up and the excitement came to a head, the winner was announced. The crown went to seventeen-year-old Rosemary La Planche, who had also been named Miss California the previous year and even made it as far as first runner-up to Miss America. The blonde, hazel-eyed beauty had refused movie offers during the past year in order to remain eligible for the 1941 contest. Unlike her 1940 bid for the top crown, Rosemary was successful in September and named Miss America, 1941. Both Jeanne and La Planche were actually too young to be eligible under the rules implemented in 1938, with eighteen being the minimum age.

Jeanne as Miss Long Beach, and 2nd Runner-up to Miss California, 1941
(Courtesy of the Jeanne Crain Brinkman Family Trust)

Although she didn't win the grand prize, Jeanne wasn't disheartened by the fact that she came in third and was pictured in her bathing suit on the front page of the *Los Angeles Times* the following morning, alongside La Planche and the second-place winner, Bernice Brady of Hollywood. The event also brought her to the attention of Ivan Kahn, a seasoned talent scout for 20th Century-Fox, whose discoveries included Linda Darnell in her native Dallas, Texas. Four days after the Miss California contest, Kahn contacted Lew Schreiber, a Fox executive and casting director, about Jeanne, reporting that he had interviewed her after the pageant and thought he might be interested in meeting her. She read a scene from *The Barretts of Wimpole Street*, which led to a screen test, a sophisticated affair from the *Ziegfeld Follies* with an evening gown and upswept hairdo to match. "Not that I fooled them much about my age," Jeanne later remembered. Her youth and inexperience worked against her and nothing came of the test, other than Kahn continued to think the young beauty queen had potential.

Shortly after the pageant, Jeanne, along with other girls who competed in the contest, were treated to a tour of RKO Pictures. Radio-Keith-Orpheum was born, according to legend, from a conversation in a Manhattan oyster bar in 1928 between famed business tycoons David Sarnoff and Joseph P. Kennedy. The smallest of the "Big Five" Hollywood studios (the remaining four including MGM, Warner Brothers, 20th Century-Fox and Paramount), RKO had showcased the talents of Katharine Hepburn and the dancing duo of Fred Astaire and Ginger Rogers throughout the 1930s. By the decade's end, Hepburn had moved on to

MGM, and Astaire and Rogers had amicably parted ways to develop their own separate careers. Enter Orson Welles.

As the 1940s began, the top brass at RKO was determined to make the studio a place where prestige pictures could be produced. Part of their plan included hiring talented newcomers who showed great promise, and this included twenty-five-year old Welles and his Mercury Theatre group. His first project at the studio was *Citizen Kane*, an artistically brilliant film that was wrought with budget and distribution problems. Its premiere was, however, a shining moment for RKO in its goal for high end movies. While still basking in the *Citizen Kane* glory, Welles began work on what would be his second project for the studio, *The Magnificent Ambersons*, a turn-of-the-century drama based on Booth Tarkington's Pulitzer Prize-winning novel.

While visiting RKO, Jeanne was lunching in the studio commissary when Welles spotted her and summoned the publicity man who was heading the girls' tour to his table. When he asked about the "girl with the red-brown, curly hair," the publicity man explained who she was. Welles asked the man to offer Jeanne an invitation to his office for tea at four o'clock that afternoon. Hardly able to contain herself the rest of the day, she met with him at the appointed time and found him charming and understanding of her nervousness. Hollywood's "boy wonder" explained that he was in the early stages of producing *The Magnificent Ambersons*, which would start shooting in September, and was looking for a girl to play Lucy Morgan, the young romantic female lead, asking if she would like to test for the role. He gave her ten pages of dialogue to memorize and instructed her to return in three days for the screen test.

In a 1917 issue of *Metropolitan* magazine the author of *The Magnificent Ambersons* gave a physical description of his characters, even more so than he had in the book. While casting his film, Welles used these descriptions to help visualize the principal characters. Tarkington described the young female in his tale as follows: "Lucy is any pretty and young cutie from Vassar or Smith: nifty clothes and brains, too."

On the allotted day Loretta accompanied her daughter to RKO, where Welles tested the nervous teen with actor Tim Holt, using a dolly shot of the two young people walking down the street while saying their lines of dialogue. When the test was completed, the director thanked her and said that he would contact her mother in a few days. When the call came through it was disappointing. Welles told Loretta that Jeanne photographed much too young for the part and "the quality he'd seen in her hadn't come through on the screen." She was either too young or too inexperienced to project it, though he did think she had possibilities and advised her to study.

Welles interviewed more than two dozen young actresses and shot eleven tests for the role of Lucy before casting Anne Baxter, who was relatively new to Hollywood, having made her movie debut a year earlier. According to Baxter's account of her casting, Welles would have preferred Jeanne: "I'd talked with and tested for Orson Welles," she recalled, "but he said his heart was set on Jeanne Crain, who he'd met in the RKO commissary. Jeanne was prettier than I was but hadn't acted as yet. RKO studio head George Shaefer made the call much to Orson's displeasure."

With the Welles reading and the Miss California contest under her belt, Jeanne went into her final year at Inglewood High primed for more experience on both the dramatic as well as the beauty pageant stage. She appeared in the senior class play, a three-act comedy titled *Ever Since Eve*, playing a Southern siren named Lucybelle Lee, and was given much encouragement by the dramatics coach, Miss Lawrence. She had overcome much of the shyness she displayed at St. Mary's and her beauty queen résumé expanded when her classmates named her Grid Queen of the 1941 football season. By the New Year she was named Miss Pan-Pacific, a title which required her to make appearances throughout southern California that winter, including the Westwood Ice Arena for local hockey games and the dedication of the first ski chair lift at Mt. Waterman.

In April 1942, as Jeanne was preparing to finish out her senior year of high school, Loretta encouraged her daughter to enter a pageant being held in Long Beach. Sponsored by the Long Beach Junior Chamber of Commerce, the "Camera Girl" contest was the fourth such event in as many years for amateur photographers in the area. Entries were submitted early, with Ann Ulmanek, a twenty-two-year old beauty from Long Beach being promoted in the local papers as the first to put her name in the hat. Although she was still only sixteen for another five and a half weeks, Jeanne claimed she was seventeen and entered the competition. The forty girls vying for the title posed for a horde of photographers along a lengthy platform set up on the beach between the Rainbow and Silver Spray piers. In a teal one-piece bathing suit and a gardenia in her long, wavy hair, Number 19, Jeanne Crain of Los Angeles was announced the winner, becoming the "Camera Girl of 1942." Ulmanek was named runner-up, which came with the title, "America's 1942 Beach Girl." As "Camera Girl," Jeanne received a trophy, a $50 war bond and both local and national exposure. The event was covered by the *LA Times*, and garnered a spot on a Movietone newsreel, which showcased a beaming, bathing suit-clad Crain in theaters across the nation.

With the exposure of the beauty pageant wins and the encouragement from Orson Welles, Loretta could see the potential in her daughter to have a long-term career in the movies. Talent scout Ivan Kahn had kept in touch with the Crains, and Loretta called him four days after the "Camera Girl" competition to say that Jeanne was planning to sign an agency contract with Walter Kane. Agents were important, and Kane was well-known in Hollywood, both for his connections, as well as being the then-husband of Twentieth Century-Fox actress Lynn Bari (the couple would separate later in 1942 and divorce the following year). Ivan spoke to Kane, explaining about the Fox test made of Jeanne the previous year and asked the agent to let him know how things developed with her. The agent promised that when he signed her, he would keep in touch, so that Fox would have the inside track if they were still interested in Jeanne as a contract player.

As a result of the "Camera Girl" contest, Jeanne met photographer William Mortensen, a juror for the competition, for whom she began modeling. Although mostly forgotten in modern circles, Mortensen worked in the pictorial style, a movement of photography which promoted the manipulation of an otherwise straightforward photograph to create an image rather than simply recording it. He became a leading pictorialist after arriving in Hollywood in 1921 at the age of twenty-four. He first came to town acting as escort to fourteen-year-old Fay Wray, with whom he became acquainted as a family friend. Fay went on to make a name for herself in the movies, most notably in *King Kong*, and Mortensen eventually opened his own photographic studio and school in Laguna Beach. His images were dark in nature, cinematic in appearance and relied heavily on sex and the occult. The photographer was reviled by mainstream artists of his field including Ansel Adams, Willard Van Dyke and others, who felt Mortensen's work "represented cheap, pictorialist sensationalism." They objected to him as "a mortal enemy of serious photography," and he became a target of their vitriol because he was finding success publishing his work and teaching his technique. When asked about his distaste for Mortensen's work, Ansel Adams replied: "[He] represented about the lowest ebb of pictorialism... It just seemed to be as far from photography as possible. He still is very popular in some circles but for us he was the anti-Christ."

Mortensen was known for his beautiful models, many who posed nude. When Jeanne began modeling for him, there were no nudes, but plenty of erotically charged cheesecake. The photographer would declare that his new muse had "the most beautiful face and the most beautiful figure in one body that I've ever seen." For the duration of their shoots, Mortensen installed the seventeen-year-old into a summer house, accompanied by both Loretta and Rita as chaperones, even paying for their meals. He became

The Mortensen Period, 1942

(Courtesy of the Jeanne Crain Brinkman Family Trust)

infatuated with his new model, though the feeling was one-sided and, like his relationship with Fay Wray, remained chaste.

Crain would later remember Mortensen as a tough but talented taskmaster and her time with him as a rewarding education. "I was pretty young then," she recalled, "and while I had rosier dreams about a career, I had very little notion about how to realize them. What Bill taught me in front of his still camera stood me in good stead later on in front of the movie camera... But truthfully, I was unprepared for the volume of shots he made of me. We worked together for something like eight months, and during that time he made over three thousand negatives of me in so many places, poses and costumes that I can't even remember them all. Because he worked fourteen hours a day, I guess he expected everyone to." Mortensen photographed Jeanne daily, reportedly shooting 3,440 poses, including sessions with her dressed as St. Bernadette of Lourdes with the intention of pitching her as a possible lead for a film version of *The Song of Bernadette*, written by Franz Werfel.

The fledgling model had come to the attention of impresario Max Reinhardt, when she enrolled in his well-known acting school in Hollywood. The famed Austrian-born theatrical producer had discovered Olivia de Havilland nearly a decade before and made her a star in his gargantuan production of Shakespeare's *A Midsummer Night's Dream*. Reinhardt had worked with Werfel several times in the past and had an option on the film rights to Werfel's bestselling novel, *Bernadette*, which had been selected as the Book-of-the-Month during the summer of 1942. After seeing Jeanne, Reinhardt was impressed by the "unlived" quality on her face. Although she read for the plum role of Bernadette, her hopes were dashed before she could make a test, when Reinhardt's plans fell through and Twentieth Century-Fox purchased the rights to film the story.

Jeanne as Saint Bernadette of Lourdes,
by William Mortensen, 1942
(Courtesy of the Jeanne Crain Brinkman Family Trust)

She did, however, attend a performance at Mr. Reinhardt's Workshop Theater, where studio talent scouts frequented, looking for fresh faces among the footlights. Also in the audience that evening was Ivan Kahn and before the evening was over two of Kahn's fellow talent scouts, Solly Biano from Warner Brothers and Milt Lewis of Paramount, also approached Jeanne with interest in a test for their respective studios. She explained that she had already spoken with Mr. Kahn, who continued to shoot memos to Fox honchos singing the girl's praises: "I think this girl is one of the best prospects in Hollywood," he wrote. "She has brains, looks and every quality to make her a box office attraction. She is star material."

Her family, both immediate and extended, certainly had their fingers crossed that things would work out successfully for their young lass. Loretta received a letter from her sister, Marie Rousseau, in the fall of 1942, wishing her niece the greatest luck in her Hollywood endeavors. "I think Jean [sic] is surely having thrilling days & experiences," she wrote. "I hope she has her chance in the movies. I pray that she will have that chance. But all this modeling isn't anything to sneeze at.... Someday, Jean will sign a rich contract."

Kahn persisted in his quest to get her noticed by the Fox front office. "This girl has real beauty and intelligence," he wrote in yet another memo. He suggested she be put under contract at $75 or $100 a week and allowed to "become a fine box office attraction," while including examples of her looks and poise from shots by Mortensen taken from a recent issue of *International Photographer* magazine.

In late 1942, Fox viewed a 16-mm color test made at RKO, and brought to them by Paul Kohner, an agent with whom Jeanne signed instead of Walter Kane. With this test, she impressed executives enough that she received and signed a contract with Twentieth Century-Fox the following

February. The financial compensation laid out in the pact was more in line with Ivan Kahn's numbers than the "rich contract" her aunt had foreseen. The standard agreement paid her $100 a week, and made Fox her professional home for a decade, as well as the place where she would gain her greatest fame. She wasn't yet eighteen.

{ 3 }
Zanuck and His Rising Star

Darryl Francis Zanuck was aptly described by *Time* magazine as a "wiry, high-domed man," gnawing on a massive cigar as he "paced back and forth and spewed memoranda in a loud Midwestern twang." The studio mogul was known as much for his forays on the casting couch as he was his personal oversight of his studio's film productions. Zanuck had worked in the motion picture industry since the early 1920s, starting out as a writer for slapstick comedy king, Mack Sennett. He then moved to Warner Brothers before forming his own studio, 20th Century Pictures, with fellow executive Joseph M. Schenck. In 1935, Zanuck and Schenck bought out the bankrupt Fox Film Corporation and merged its resources with their own to become Twentieth Century-Fox.

By 1941, he was one of the biggest bosses in Tinsel Town, on par with Louis B. Meyer at MGM and Jack Warner at Warner Brothers. Yet, when the United States entered World War II at the end of the year, Zanuck sought military service and was commissioned as a colonel in the Army Signal Corps. In September 1942, he was granted leave from the studio to devote his full attention to military affairs, and was stationed, among other places, in North Africa. By the end of May, 1943, he received permission to go on inactive duty, and resumed his standing at Fox.

When he returned from service, Zanuck wanted to meet with the new studio talent that had been signed on while he was away. Jeanne hadn't done much since coming on board at Twentieth Century-Fox. In the spring, she attended the sidewalk ceremony at Grauman's Chinese of curmudgeon actor Monty Woolley, along with fellow beauty queen Jo-Carroll Dennison. Acting as studio window dressing, the two comely young women assisted Woolley in imprinting his famous beard into the wet cement. The same month as the Woolley publicity, she, along with three other young starlets, appeared in Los Angeles superior court as minors, seeking approval of their motion picture contracts, since they were underage.

Successful in her effort, she signed a long-term pact with the studio in early June, in lieu of her standard contract. Later that year she made her movie debut in a Technicolor musical extravaganza called *The Gang's All Here*, which starred Fox veteran Alice Faye. Wearing a bathing suit and flower in her hair (just as she had done winning the "Camera Girl" competition), she uttered a single line of dialogue to Charlotte Greenwood. It was an inauspicious introduction to motion pictures but it would be the only time in her screen career that she didn't play a significant role in a film.

Along with the other young hopefuls at Fox, Jeanne was summoned to the studio to meet with her new boss. Coming in from the beach, she was suntanned and wore slacks and her hair in a kerchief. During her interview Zanuck asked her age and where she went to school. When he discovered she knew French, he spoke it to her and she felt at ease when he asked her to stand up and walk around the room to see what she looked like. She asked him about her hair, because people had told her she wore it too long. He instructed her not to change it at all. "I like you as you are," he replied. He then said he wanted her to test for a part in *Home in*

Indiana, an upcoming picture about rural life on a horse farm, and gave her the script. Impressed by her wholesome beauty, Zanuck cast her as Char, a pretty tomboy who liked horses and the new boy next door, played by Lon McCallister. Along with Jeanne and McCallister, the film would feature another fresh face, June Haver, who had also made her debut in a bit role in *The Gang's All Here*. Jeanne and June were

The 1943 Starlet Brigade: Fox hopefuls (l-r), Mary Anderson, June Haver, Gale Robbins, Jeanne, and Trudy Marshall. Only Haver and Crain would hit the bigtime at the studio.

just two of the new Fox starlets being promoted as "Stars of Tomorrow" upon Zanuck's return, a striking bunch which also included Mary Anderson, Gale Robbins and Trudy Marshall. The studio had found success with horse racing pictures in the past, namely *Kentucky* in 1938 and *Maryland* in 1940, so, in 1941, it was looking to duplicate this lucrative formula with a film set in Indiana. John Payne, an up-and-coming star at Fox, Walter Brennan and Fay Bainter, all actors who had appeared in *Maryland*, were slated for the new project. By 1942, however, the direction of the picture had changed and the film rights to another horse story were acquired. *The Phantom Filly* was a 1941 novel by George Agnew Chamberlain, which first appeared as a serial in *The Saturday Evening Post*. Afraid a film with phantom in the title would be mistaken for a horror picture, the movie became *Home in Indiana*, and began production in mid-September, 1943.

Jeanne and Lon McCallister spent two weeks on a Santa Barbara ranch learning the proper manner of handling driving horses. The two young people became friends and it wasn't long before the publicity department began connecting them socially. Lon had been appearing in movies since the mid-1930s as an uncredited bit player in juvenile roles, including quick stints in George Cukor's *Romeo and Juliet* at MGM, and *The Adventures of Tom Sawyer* for David O. Selznick. He made an impression as a star-struck serviceman in the morale-boosting wartime musical, *Stage Door Canteen* (1943) before being cast in *Home in Indiana*.

As Sparke Thornton, McCallister plays a juvenile delinquent who is sent to live with his aunt and uncle on their farm. Just as he decides to run away he discovers a neighboring horse farm, as well as two cute local girls, the pretty and down-to-earth Char (Jeanne) and blond glamour puss Cri-Cri (June Haver). Sparke finds rehabilitation through his love of harness racing and the friendships he makes along his way. The film's director, Henry Hathaway, was able to persuade Zanuck to allow him to take cast and crew and shoot on location in the nation's Middle West. Much of the rural landscapes and race track shots were filmed at various spots in Ohio and Kentucky, though autumn arrived sooner than Technicolor crews would have liked and barrels of green paint were ordered from Hollywood to spray the surrounding trees and grass back to their spring hues. Jeanne and other cast members traveled east for fifty-four days of location shooting and spent much of their free time at local war bond rallies, military hospitals and war plants.

Other than her tiny bit part in *The Gang's All Here*, Jeanne was a complete newcomer to the world of filmmaking. When she appeared on the set of *Home in Indiana* looking the way she thought a film actress should, veteran director Hathaway set her straight. "She was plastered with lipstick," he recalled, "her hair was set, and I spotted a cap on a front tooth. I took out my handkerchief and wiped off the makeup, combed out and braided her hair, and yanked off the cap. Then I said, 'Look, you're just a kid, and this is just a kid you're playing. Be yourself.'" Later, as filming progressed on location, Hathaway wired Darryl Zanuck: "Better raise this girl's salary – she's going to be a star!"

Back in Hollywood, while she continued working on

Home in Indiana, Zanuck cast Jeanne in her first starring role in an upcoming picture called *I Married a Soldier*. Although shooting for the new project was scheduled to begin the week before Christmas 1943, the production was delayed until after the holiday because Jeanne was wrapping up her part on the *Indiana* set. *I Married a Soldier* went by many titles throughout its production, beginning with *Paris, Tennessee*, then *Army Wives*, and finally ended up as *In the Meantime, Darling*. Originally intended for director Archie Mayo, Zanuck finally assigned the film to Otto Preminger to not only direct, but produce as well, the first time the filmmaker would take on the dual task. Although it was administered from Fox's B-unit, Preminger wanted to prove himself. If he succeeded on this film, it would boost his standing on another project, *Laura*, which he had been developing as a potential picture before Zanuck's return to the studio from war duty.

In the Meantime, Darling, a patriotic comedy-drama of wartime brides, cast Jeanne as a spoiled young newlywed who comes from a wealthy family and has to adjust to living in a military boarding house with other war brides. The film not only revolved around Jeanne's character, it was also the first in which she received top billing. Fox was grooming its pretty contract player for full-fledged A-list stardom. After filming was completed in early 1944, script revisions and retakes were made in an effort to enhance her presence in the movie. Austrian-born Preminger found his young star's "wholesome, beauty queen veneer" appealing and he directed her gently, "appreciating her serene temperament [and] lack of inner fire." He didn't, however, confuse these traits with her desire for a Hollywood career, saying: "In my opinion Jeanne Crain has more chance to become and remain a star than anybody I have met in recent years, because of her gift for concentration and her earnest will to work with only one aim in mind — perfection."

The film wasn't without its share of controversy. In his autobiography, Preminger recalled an incident with Eugene Pallette, a popular character actor who was playing Jeanne's father, which led to the actor's dismissal from the picture. According to Preminger, Pallette was "an admirer of Hitler and convinced that Germany would win the war." The trouble on the set began, however, when the actor refused to sit at the same table as an African-American actor named Clarence Muse. When instructed to enter the scene and take a seat at the kitchen table beside Muse, Pallette reportedly proclaimed to the director: "You're out of your mind. I won't sit next to a nigger." Preminger went immediately to Zanuck and had Pallette fired and his remaining scenes removed from the picture. The actor's career did indeed end only two years after the release of *In the Meantime, Darling* but oddly, in 1953, Palette was one of the guests at a banquet honoring Madame Sul-Te-Wan, an elderly African-American actress with whom he had appeared in the silent classic, *The Birth of a Nation,* in 1915.

There was also concern from Joseph Breen's office at the Production Code Administration about a scene where Crain and co-star Frank Latimore, as the young newlyweds, share the same bed. The final cut of the film did show the young couple on a joint matrimonial mattress and Preminger would later recall with satisfaction: "There was much excitement because for the first time in films, the Code permitted us to show married people in the same bed." The Legion of

Decency, always combating objectionable material in motion pictures, gave it an A-2 classification, suitable for adults.

By the end of 1943, Jeanne's name was starting to show up in the top movie magazines and newspapers across the country, as a rising starlet as well as for promotion of the yet to be released *Home in Indiana*. As a major impetus of her daughter's blossoming career, Loretta felt a sense of pride when she received a Christmas card from Texas friends exclaiming their excitement about Jeanne's rising celebrity. "[We] are so happy for your good fortune and can hardly wait for Jeanne's picture to come to town," wrote Opal Garvin. "Did you know there was a newspaper picture of her recently in the *Dallas Times Herald*? What a happy surprise that was, to pick up the evening paper and see our little Jeanne!"

Having two major feature films in post-production with her name prominently displayed in the credits was a boon to her professional reputation, and her amount of quality publicity increased dramatically in 1944. As a sign of her rising stock at the studio, despite not having a picture released yet, she was given Sonja Henie's dressing room, when the skating film star's contract ended. She emerged as one of Zanuck's favorites of the new wave of hires at Fox, not in the way of Carole Landis, who was one of the producer's many four o'clock trysts, but in a protective, encouraging way, like a favorite daughter. She was invited to the Zanuck home for dinner on the night of the *Home in Indiana* preview and, much to her excitement, met such Tinsel Town heavyweights as famed celebrity hostess Elsa Maxwell, the Samuel Goldwyns and Cary Grant and his wife, heiress Barbara Hutton. When *Home in Indiana* was finally released in June it was promoted with an extensive advertising

Jeanne with Twentieth Century-Fox boss, Darryl F. Zanuck and his children. Columnist Louella Parsons looks on in the background.

campaign. Premieres of the movie were set to be held between June 14-28 in 193 theaters in Indiana, Ohio, Illinois and Kentucky with state and municipal authorities, as well as Jeanne and June Haver appearing at some of the half dozen openings. It was an exciting time for Crain, who had never been outside California before her experiences with filming and promoting the feature.

The world premiere was held at the aptly named Indiana theater in Indianapolis and was tied in with the state's war bond activities. Jeanne, with her mother close by, was present for a personal appearance which was covered by a net of publicity, including local and regional daily papers, national news wires and radio coverage in key cities across the state. The publicity not only helped promote the film but also benefited its new young star by putting her name in American households. A massive war bond rally, built around the premiere in Indianapolis, attracted thousands and brought in over $7,000,000, including funds collected from the auction of a three and one-half month-old thoroughbred filly registered under the name *Jeanne Crain*.

Along with June Haver, Jeanne arrived in Indianapolis two days before the premiere. The two starlets were met at the station by a military guard of honor who escorted them to the lobby of the depot, where a special radio hook up allowed them to be interviewed. They were then taken, in Army jeeps, to their hotel. The following morning the girls were again interviewed by the press at an informal breakfast and June departed for Cincinnati, where she had lived as a girl, for that city's premiere. Jeanne remained in Indianapolis, and visited the Two Gait Farm, where she was photographed with her namesake, the young filly. The following day she toured the local Army base, Fort Benjamin Harrison, and Billings Hospital, serving food to recuperating GIs and eating a meal with them. She met back up with Haver in Cleveland, Ohio on the morning of that city's premiere and went through yet another whirlwind of publicity. More interviews were followed by a ride on an Army amphibious duck in Lake Erie. Film related stops in Kentucky included Louisville and Lexington. After all the hoopla subsided, the two stars made their way back to California, enjoying a layover in Chicago to celebrate Haver's belated birthday at the Ambassador Hotel.

Home in Indiana was a hit with box-office receipts coming in at $1.75 million. Jeanne's contributions and popularity in the movie did not go unrecognized and by the end of June, she was given a new contract with Fox which offered her star billing and a salary raise to $250 a week. She was also announced to have a starring role in an upcoming picture called *Leave Her to Heaven*. By autumn, the appeal of *Home in Indiana* was still swirling with audiences, and in early October, Crain appeared with her *Indiana* costars, Walter Brennan, Charlotte Greenwood and June Haver in a 60-minute radio broadcast of the movie on the "Lux Radio Theater."

Audiences weren't as enamored with *In the Meantime, Darling*, which premiered in September. Neither were reviewers, who gave the light comedy-drama, and Crain's performance in it, a lukewarm reception at best. *Film Daily* noted that "Jeanne Crain's first starring vehicle isn't the best of sendoffs, although the girl performs sympathetically." *Variety* was like-minded in its criticism, stating: "Twentieth-Fox is giving its new femme lead, Jeanne Crain, a star buildup, but neither her first vehicle nor her performance in it, gets her off to an auspicious start." The reviewer went on to say, the "wavering story may be partly responsible for Miss Crain's unconvincing performance, but she needs plenty more training and work before she rates the stellar billing Twentieth has given her." It ended up on the lower half of a double bill with another low-budget Fox programmer, *Sweet and Lowdown*, which starred Lynn Bari and Linda Darnell.

Despite the weak reception for *In the Meantime, Darling*, Fox continued to have big plans in store for its young starlet. As early as May, even before the release of *Home in Indiana*, the studio had bought the rights to Dale Eunson's novel, *Our Moment is Swift*, as a starring vehicle for Crain. It was a story of youthful, wartime marriage which never made it to the screen. *Bon Voyage* was another much-anticipated picture in which Jeanne was to star. It was announced in August that she would share the screen with Anne Baxter, Joan Blondell and Joan Bennett in a tale of women on the home front during World War II based on Josephine Lawrence's best-selling novel *A Tower of Steel*. When production began in October, Baxter and Bennett were out and Fox contract star Lynn Bari was signed on. Jeanne was cast in the lead role of Bon, a seventeen-year-old taking on her first full-time job in a law office. Acclaimed stage director Lee Strasberg of the New York Theatre Guild had been at Twentieth Century-Fox for six months learning film technique when he was assigned *Bon Voyage* as his first picture. After a week of shooting, however, Zanuck pulled the plug on the film, and Strasberg, whose direction was slow, failed to gain traction as a movie director and eventually returned to New York.

In late October 1944, Fox announced plans for a remake of *The Farmer Takes a Wife*, which had been filmed nearly a decade before with Janet Gaynor and Henry Fonda. Jeanne was named to the Gaynor part and producer Robert Bassler hoped that by the time the picture was underway, Lon McCallister would be out of the Army and able to take on the Fonda role. Just as the other projects announced for her that summer, *The Farmer Takes a Wife* was shelved although it would be dusted off several years later as a musical starring

Betty Grable. Jeanne's next picture would, however, feature her once again with McCallister.

Winged Victory was a successful stage play written by popular playwright Moss Hart, as a tribute to the American Army Air Forces. When Fox planned to bring the popular play to the screen, Zanuck personally produced the picture, and William Wyler was scheduled to direct it. When Wyler was called away to Washington for war work, Fox borrowed George Cukor from MGM to direct, and hired most of the Broadway cast, actors who were also actual servicemen, to appear in the film version. Lon was the exception. He was cast in the lead because Fox wanted to ensure good box-office, as well as keep McCallister's name relevant for the time he would be off-screen for military service. At the request of the studio, Lon was transferred from cryptography school in the Signal Corps to the set of *Winged Victory*.

Although they weren't coupled in the film (Crain was Barry Sullivan's girl this time), Jeanne and Lon continued to be linked together in newspaper items and movie magazines. Columnist Walter Winchell had the two young contract stars "madly in love" with each other, but McCallister replied to the claim that neither of them had "even thought of such a thing," saying "Jeanne is a wonderful girl and I like her very much. We've been out on a few dates together. She spent one weekend at my house." He was referring to his Malibu beach house, but just to make sure that no hanky-panky was insinuated he reiterated that they were most definitely not alone. "Several people from the wardrobe and makeup department of 20th [Century-Fox] were there-and so were my folks-my mother, grandmother and grandfather." So much for a romantic rendezvous. In actuality, McCallister was homosexual and romantically linked with fellow Fox newcomer William Eythe. Nonetheless, Lon and Jeanne continued to be photographed and written about as Hollywood's freshest and most wholesome young couple, even attending the world premiere of the prestigious Fox production, *Wilson* in New York with Darryl Zanuck and other studio luminaries. McAllister made it clear though, when he said: "The premiere of *Wilson* was the first planned date we've ever had... but as far as any real dates were concerned, we just didn't have any."

Winged Victory was a success for Zanuck and, although her role was secondary as one of the women on the home front, a boost for Crain's fledgling career. During filming, director George Cukor encouraged the young actress about her future films. "You've shown remarkable progress in a short time, Jeanne," he said. "You should begin to study with some good teacher." She enjoyed working with Cukor who taught her so many things, like "how to cry from inside, which she'd never been able to do, because she'd never had very much to cry about." Taking the acclaimed director's advice, Jeanne began a daily, two-hour drama lesson from Madame Ludmilla Pitoeff, a noted European actress who had recently appeared on Broadway and was currently at Fox. Her hard work and focus paid off and she began to gain a reputation as "one-take Crain."

Jeanne wasn't just working hard at honing her acting skills. In late 1944, the studio was promoting her career aggressively, publishing trade advertisement which challenged industry insiders to "remember the names" of Jeanne Crain, Vivian Blaine, June Haver, William Eythe and its new singing star Dick Haymes. She began to appear on the same covers of Hollywood's top fan magazines, in whose pages and columns she had appeared frequently the previous year. She continued personal appearances promoting her films including a trip to San Diego in late December to christen a B-24 Liberator bomber aircraft bearing the name *Winged Victory*. Everything was going so fast and so well for her since joining Twentieth Century-Fox, but her career was at a point that she could continue on being just another starlet, or hit her stride with a big break.

The studio had revived interest in a screenplay that had been shuffled around since 1940 called *Miss Pilgrim's Progress*, with plans to cast Jeanne in the lead role as the first woman typist, but it continued on the back burner until it was given to Betty Grable in 1947. Although Crain had been announced for one of the main roles in the upcoming *Leave Her to Heaven*, it was fellow Fox beauty Gene Tierney who would garner most of the attention there. Then, in early November 1944, the studio released the announcement that Jeanne had been given the lead in its musical remake of *State Fair*. It was career gold. *State Fair* was to be a big Technicolor production and one of the studio's largest projects of the new year. It would also propel Crain into the echelons of true stardom at Fox.

{ 4 }
Twentieth Century-Fox Presents "The Girl Next Door"

As 1945 began, Elsa Maxwell, professional hostess and bastion of society and gossip, predicted that before year's end, Jeanne would be "right up in the front ranks of top-notch stars." She went even further to claim the young actress would "be *the* star of the New Year" with some of the same "qualities that made Jennifer [Jones] a star with her first picture, [The Song of] *Bernadette*." Circumstances were certainly aligning for her prediction to come to pass.

In the summer of 1943, Fox was contemplating a remake of its box-office hit, *State Fair*, made a decade earlier. The original film had co-starred homespun humorist Will Rogers and wholesome Janet Gaynor in a popular filmization of a bestselling book by native Iowan Phil Stong. Despite the squeaky-clean image presented by its many film incarnations, Stong's novel presented the youthful love found along the midway to be less than chaste, "a surprisingly dark coming-of-age story that took as its major plot device the effects of the 'worldly temptations' of the Iowa State Fair on a local farming family." Both of the youthful main characters, rural brother and sister Wayne and Margy Frake, lose their virginity to their respective suitors within days of arriving at the much-celebrated State Fair, a plot point which caused Stong's hometown library in Keosauqua, Iowa to ban his book. The '33 movie version doesn't suggest that Gaynor's Margy has taken the big step, however, when Wayne is besotted with a shapely lady trapeze artist, who gives him his first alcoholic drink and seduces him, he tells his family that he spent the night before with a male friend. His father observes that Wayne should pay rent, as he's been "sleepin' with that fella for three nights," to which his mother adds, "I'll bet you boys just fool around and don't get a wink of sleep." These tidbits of dialogue slipped through the censors but the suggestive scene between Wayne and his gal pal did not, and was cut in post-Code re-release (Post-code was the period after 1934 when censorship restrictions were strictly adhered to in Hollywood).

Jeanne with Dana Andrews in *State Fair* (1945)
It would be their first of four films together.

With the production code in full force by 1943, subject matter of seduction and in-tact virginity would be moot points for any potential remake. Also, Zanuck wanted to add music to the folksy story, which would lend to the wholesome atmosphere he wanted to reflect with war-time audiences.

Songwriters Richard Rodgers and Oscar Hammerstein II traveled west from New York that July to discuss with Zanuck the potential of transforming the homespun comedy-drama into a musical. The initial plan was to cast current middle-aged sensation Monty Wooley and leggy Fox star Betty Grable in the lead roles. Some East Coast insiders saw the Rodgers and Hammerstein assignment as a screen test of sorts for their own current Broadway show, *Oklahoma!* which had become a smash hit. The rationale was that a successful version of *State Fair* would increase the chances of a film version of *Oklahoma!* for which they were asking $500,000. With hectic schedules in New York, trying to get their own separate shows off the ground (Rodgers was working on *A Connecticut Yankee* and Hammerstein was adapting *Carmen Jones* from the Bizet opera), the songwriting duo wouldn't be able to start on the Fox project until late in 1943. They also made it clear that they wanted to work on the project on the East coast. In his autobiography, Rodgers explained that both he and Hammerstein were adamant on this point.

> "We made sure, though, that our contract included one provision. Because of our multiple activities in New York, we had no intention of spending an extended length of time in Hollywood, and we insisted that we be allowed to write the songs in the East. Though they found the request a bit unusual, the studio people agreed; the story, which was set in Iowa, would be filmed in California, while the music and lyrics would be written in Fairfield Connecticut, and Doylestown, Pennsylvania [where Rodgers and Hammerstein, respectively, resided]"

It would be a full year before a finished and revised script was submitted, and in the meantime, Fox began casting the picture. The initial names of Wooley and Grable were scrapped and longtime Fox musical star Alice Faye was suggested for the role of band singer Emily Edwards, who had been written as the world-wise trapeze artist in the earlier film. Faye would instead go into production for her first dramatic role in the studio's moody film noir, *Fallen Angel*, the last film she would make before retiring from motion pictures at the age of thirty. In late October, 1944, Faye's *Fallen Angel* co-star, Dana Andrews was cast, as the street-smart, big city reporter with whom Margy Frake falls in love. The same month, singer Dick Haymes, Fox's answer to Sinatra, was signed on to play Wayne, the singing son of the Frake family, and negotiations were taking place with Metro-Goldwyn-Mayer to borrow Kathryn Grayson, that studio's resident soprano. Instead, Vivian Blaine was cast as the warm and warbling Emily, with Charles Winniger and Fay Bainter rounding out the main cast as the Frake parents. Walter Lang was assigned to direct this colorful crew and Jeanne made wardrobe tests the week of Christmas, 1944 with primary filming beginning the next month.

The Rodgers and Hammerstein score, their first and only written exclusively for the movie screen, was filled with soulful and energetic songs, including "It Might as Well Be Spring." It was a showcase for Jeanne during the first minutes of the film, though she was dubbed by vocalist Louanne Hogan, who had been signed by Fox to sing specifically for its star. *Variety* would later comment on Jeanne's "excellent singing voice," not realizing that it was Hogan they were hearing. In February, pleased with her continued success, Fox renewed Crain's contract. Shooting wrapped on *State Fair* in late March, and the busy actress then appeared in the *All-Star Bond Rally*, a two-reel short film produced by Fox in conjunction with the War Activities Committee and the U.S. Treasury Department to promote the sale of war bonds. Jeanne played herself, a pin-up come to life for an overseas serviceman (ironically played by her *In the Meantime, Darling* co-star, Frank Latimore). Her spot lasted less than ten seconds but allowed her to have her name in the credits along with stalwarts of the business including Bob Hope, Bing Crosby and Betty Grable.

In her next picture, she would share top-billing with her equally famous costars, though her name would come third. Fox was negotiating the purchase of the film rights for *Leave Her to Heaven* in May 1944, even before the novel had been published. Encouraged by writer Joseph Mankiewicz, and directors John Stahl and Otto Preminger, Zanuck paid $100,000 for Ben Ames Williams' story, with plans to star Tallulah Bankhead and Ida Lupino in the lead female roles. Williams' book would go on to become one of the top sellers of the year and a successful screen adaptation was highly anticipated. In November, Bankhead told friends that she wouldn't appear in the film, adding, "I've played all kinds of slitches, but I'll be darned if I do a murderess." Tallulah failed to mention, however, that Zanuck had already assigned the part of Ellen to sultry studio beauty, Linda Darnell, after seeing daily rushes of her in the dark melodrama, *Hangover Square*. By December, Paulette Goddard was mentioned as the lucky actress to be given the lead role, followed in the gossip columns by Joan Fontaine. Just after the New Year, it was announced that Gene Tierney would play the coveted part. The actress had been at Fox since 1940, portraying exotic vamps and cool ice queens before scoring a huge hit with *Laura*, a sophisticated mystery, costarring Dana Andrews. Although Jeanne was announced for the role of sweet and innocent Ruth early in the casting process, Fox newcomer Faye Marlowe was "penciled in for the role of the good sister," but Crain would prevail and she and Tierney would share the screen with one of the studio's new leading men, Cornel Wilde.

Jeanne Crain and her sister, Rita, enjoy scenery on "Leave Her To Heaven" location.

Jeanne and Rita on location at Bass Lake for
Leave Her to Heaven, 1945
Screenland Magazine, October 1945

Leave Her to Heaven was a psychological thriller of the highest order. Its main character, Ellen Berent, is a sleek and beautiful, yet selfish and manipulative creature, who woos and marries an unsuspecting writer, Richard Harland

(Wilde). In the course of their marriage, she lets Harland's crippled brother drown in a lake, throws herself down a staircase in an attempt to abort their unborn child (whom she feels will replace her in her husband's affections) and finally kills herself with poison, while making it appear that her innocent adopted sister, Ruth, did the dirty deed. The film's director, John Stahl, shot the picture in lush, crayon-coated Technicolor, making the taut melodrama even more visually tantalizing.

Production began in late May, 1945, and due to a studio strike, organized by the Confederation of Studio Unions (CSU), the cameras rolled at Bass Lake, nestled in the High Sierras of northern California, instead of the Fox lot. Gene Tierney reported for work only three days after completing her most recent picture, *Dragonwyck* (although this film would actually be released after *Leave Her to Heaven*). She reflected on her experience of making the movie in her 1979 autobiography, *Self-Portrait*.

> "*Leave Her to Heaven* was not an easy film to make. The really good ones seldom are. We went on location to Arizona and to Bass Lake in northern California, and there were long, anxious drives each morning, along roads that seemed to have a precipice at every corner. At one point I had to swim in an icy mountain lake in November, and was pulled out and given nips of whiskey between shots to keep my circulation going. On location, I enjoyed the company of a lovely young actress in one of her first roles, Jeanne Crain. She played my younger sister and did a fine job.

Cornel Wilde literally came from one movie set to the next. The actor had made three period pictures in a row. He finished up *The Bandit of Sherwood Forest,* at Columbia Studios, at six o'clock in the evening, then stopped at a barber shop for his first modern haircut in two years, and finally made his way to the Fox lot for *Leave Her to Heaven.* Later that night, a limousine drove him 400 miles to the High Sierras for location filming. Jeanne celebrated her twentieth birthday on the shoot and her sister, Rita, who was now attending UCLA, would join her on location and act as her stand-in.

By mid-summer, Crain's movie slate was full. Shooting of *Leave Her to Heaven* was still in progress when it was announced that she would star in an upcoming musical called *Centennial Summer.* Also, *State Fair* was ready to be released and when it was previewed in early August, it was such a smash success that the audience "almost tore the roof off the Pasadena theater." The world premiere was held in Des Moines at the end of the month, with much pomp and circumstance involved, in the same way local festivities ushered in the premiere for *Home in Indiana.* Parades, street carnivals, broadcasts and beauty contests all helped celebrate the musical extravaganza, which was shown at both the Paramount and the Des Moines Theaters to sold-out audiences.

Getting major play during the Labor Day weekend, *State Fair* was a huge hit, with Zanuck claiming it "the most popular musical we have had in years and the business nationwide is just sensational." As an added bonus for Jeanne, her musical spotlight in the film, "It Might As Well Be Spring," won the Academy Award as the year's Best Song.

The movie was an unmitigated success and it propelled Crain to stardom at Fox, as well as boosting her status in Hollywood. When she ran into her youthful crush, Gregory Peck, in Westwood Village, she commented to the actor how much she enjoyed Ingrid Bergman, with whom he had just started filming *Spellbound*. "Yes," replied Peck, "she's lovely. They call her the Jeanne Crain of the Selznick lot."

With the triumph of *State Fair*, she was number two in a list of "Stars of Tomorrow," according to a poll taken in autumn of 1945, by movie exhibitors for the trade publication, *Motion Picture Herald*. In sequence, the rising players were Dane Clark, Crain, Keenan Wynn, Peggy Ann Garner, Cornel Wilde, Tom Drake, Lon McCallister, Diana Lynn, Marilyn Maxwell and William Eythe. The announcement noted that "Jeanne Crain has beauty and ability and ambition, and her bosses pick out good roles for her. So she should be around Hollywood parts for a lucrative spell." Indeed, Zanuck recognized Jeanne's contribution to the success of *State Fair*, and this resulted in yet another new and financially significant seven-year contract in September.

1945 had been an extremely busy year for the rising young star, and her roster of potential movie titles continued to grow. In March, while *State Fair* was shooting, Fox producer William Perlberg contemplated reteaming Crain with Dana Andrews in a Technicolor remake of another old Fox subject, *Cameo Kirby*, which had been a hit for silent star, John Gilbert in 1923. In the summer, it was announced that Jeanne would co-star with Gregory Peck in a remake of 1933's *Berkeley Square*, and in September she would be paired with studio heartthrob John Payne as the romantic leads in *City of Flowers*. None of these features were produced with Jeanne in them, though *Berkeley Square* was eventually made in 1951 with Tyrone Power and Ann Blyth under the title *I'll Never Forget You,* and *City of Flowers* became *Carnival in Costa Rica*, a rather dismal Technicolor dud with Vera-Ellen and Dick Haymes. Instead, Crain continued to be part of the studio's top productions, most recently as Ruth in the glossy, *Leave Her to Heaven*, which was released in mid-December.

The premiere was a gala event hosting the elite of society, stage, screen, radio and politics at the Carthay Circle Theatre in Los Angeles. Three to four thousand fans gathered on Wednesday night, December 19, to watch their favorite celebrities arrive on the red carpet, with six searchlights brightening the sky. It was one of the biggest premieres since the war. The largest ovation went out to a star who didn't even appear in *Leave Her to Heaven*. Tyrone Power, recently returned from military duty and in his new civilian suit, received the most cheers, with Cornel Wilde, the leading man of the picture, winning the second loudest applause. In addition to the two actors, the theater was studded with moguls and A-list celebrities. The Darryl Zanucks were, of course, in attendance. Lana Turner was there with her escort, Robert Hutton, and June Haver was joined by another Fox star, Victor Mature. The notices were kind to both of the film's female stars, with *The Film Daily* claiming: "Miss Tierney has never shown to finer advantage, nor had Miss Crain," and about Jeanne specifically, Campbell Dixon, wrote in the *Daily Telegraph*: "... she will go straight to the top. She has youth and beauty, charm and breeding — four aces given to few."

As kind as the critics were to the film's stars, the box-office was even better to Zanuck and the studio, with *Leave Her to Heaven* making more money than "any Fox picture up to that time by a wide margin." Amidst all the glitz and glamour of the exhilarating premiere evening was Jeanne. She had risen swiftly in the ranks at Fox, thanks to her exquisite beauty, petite figure and guidance from Darryl Zanuck. *State Fair* had made her a star and *Leave Her to Heaven* paved the way for other, more successful pictures that she would add to her movie resume. Oh, and she had a date on that cold, December night. More than just a casual date, in fact. Someone with whom she had spent a lot of time over the past two years. He was tall, dark and very handsome. His name was Paul Brinkman.

{5}
Paul

Since making a name for herself at Fox, Jeanne's life remained relatively normal. Her grandmother, Anna Carr, died in 1944, and the Crain women moved into a small, white house on Glenrock Avenue in Westwood, a purchase made after the studio contract was signed. It was near UCLA, where Rita was enrolled, studying Psychology. The sisters would regularly talk over their respective day, Jeanne about goings on at the studio and Rita about her college adventures. It was a normal home, down to the little wire-haired fox terrier named Terry. The household focus, however, was centered on Jeanne's film career. When her daughter was working on a movie, Loretta would have no trouble getting her up at five-thirty in the morning, but it was a challenge to get her out of bed at eleven o'clock when she wasn't.

Since she was under twenty-one, California law automatically placed fifty percent of her earnings into trust (which was invested in War Bonds), twenty-two percent was paid for taxes, and ten percent to her agent. This left little in the way of personal money on which to live. Theirs was a one-car household and Mrs. Crain would drive Jeanne to the studio every morning when she was working on a picture and pick her up at the end of the day, keeping the "prowling studio wolves" at bay. The new starlet's social life was carefully regulated by her mother. Even when there was a Fox related event for which the studio wanted its young contract player to make a professional appearance date, Loretta would be consulted first.

Jeanne's name would pop up occasionally in social and gossip columns, as well as movie magazines, being squired around town by eligible bachelors, usually young contract players, and often set up by the studio. Her "romance" with Lon McCallister continued to be fodder for the fan magazines throughout 1944 and 1945. In November 1944, her named was linked with Dean Harens, a young Broadway actor who had just made his movie debut in Universal's noir, *Christmas Holiday*. Henry King, Jr., the son of one of Fox's top directors, and young actor Rory Calhoun, just getting his start in pictures, were her escorts at premieres and nightclubs. But one date showed up in print and by her side more often than the others.

Paul Brinkman was an engineer by trade and a manufacturer of plastics during the war. In 1943, he was twenty-five years-old and on the verge of a minor acting career in the movies. Born in San Francisco, he was raised in a comfortable household, in the exclusive, affluent neighborhood, St. Francis Wood. His father, Fred, had started out as part owner in a tire company, then opened an automobile dealership for the Stevens-Duryea company, and finally became a financier of cars as the president of the Royal Finance Company in San Francisco. As a small boy, Paul was sent to his mother's native England to attend boarding school. His parents had a second child in 1930, a son they named Peter. After graduation from Lowell High School in 1936, Paul attended the University of California, Berkeley, where he was a member of the Delta Kappa Epsilon fraternity. The Depression, as it had for so many, caused

61

financial ruin for Fred, and by 1940, the Brinkmans had moved to Los Angeles, where Paul worked part-time as a phonograph salesman. He was the proverbial tall, dark and handsome young man and he bore more than a passing resemblance to Errol Flynn, who had hit his prime by the early 1940s as the top male star at Warner Brothers.

Paul Brinkman, aka Paul Brooke or Brooks, young hopeful at Warner Brothers, 1944

Brinkman eventually became involved in the aircraft industry and his good looks brought him to the attention of Hollywood. His name began popping up in the gossip columns as a regular escort of pretty young starlets around Tinsel Town. If he wasn't at the Mocambo with Mary Hay Barthelmess (daughter of screen star Richard Barthelmess), he was spotted at the Beverly Tropics with June Long, only to be at the Tropics the following month squiring Ginger Rogers. In the summer of 1942 he was seen out, more than once, with exotic star June Duprez, but by late winter he and big band singer Ginny Simms were "an item all over again." As he was seen more and more around town, and his reputation as a ladies-man grew, he began being referred to as "the poor man's Errol Flynn." He looked so much like Flynn that autograph seekers would constantly approach him in public, thinking he was the mustachioed star.

Brinkman met Jeanne for the first time at the home of publicist Marshall Kester and his wife Bernice, Bobbie to her friends, during a Sunday brunch in 1943. Mrs. Kester introduced the two young people along with their respective dates. Polite amenities crossed between them and the party broke up after the hosts showed some 16-mm home movies. Then, one afternoon a few months later, Jeanne and Loretta were driving down Sunset Boulevard in Hollywood, with Mrs. Crain at the wheel. While stopped at a traffic light, Brinkman pulled up to the passenger side of their car in a sleek convertible. They made eye contact and each remembered the other, though neither could remember the other's name. The enthusiastic young man would later confess to Jeanne that he dropped behind them to catch the license plate number in an ill-fated attempt to locate her name (the Los

Angeles Traffic Bureau wouldn't oblige his request). Crain later recalled how the two finally met yet a third time.

> "My mother and sister and I went to the Farmers' Market for lunch, and while I was standing at the spaghetti counter someone behind me suddenly said, 'Hello, there! I know you,' he said, 'and I've just remembered where I met you. It was at Marshall Kester's. But I don't remember your name.' I laughed, recalling the introduction, but I admitted I'd forgotten his name, too. Naturally, we introduced ourselves all over again that day, and when he asked for my telephone number I gladly gave it to him."

She was leaving shortly after the Farmer's Market meeting, however, for location shooting on *Home in Indiana*. Jeanne spent the majority of the fall filming the movie, both in the Midwest and at the studio, so she and Paul didn't have a chance to meet again until late in the year. Their first official date was on New Year's Eve, 1943, when Paul took her to a Watch Party hosted by oil millionaire Tex Feldman. At midnight, there was champagne and singing of Auld Lang Syne, then the couple kissed. "I was wearing a white taffeta dress embroidered in gold," Jeanne recalled, "and I felt so grown up." Besides his handsome looks and good manners, Jeanne was impressed with Brinkman's ease at meeting people and his skill at conversation, which countered her own quiet manner. "I'm shy," she said, "I make only a few friends, and I'm a dreamer who hates the practical side of almost everything."

They dated on an off for a while, with Paul also seeing up-and-coming starlet and Mickey Rooney's ex-wife, Ava Gardner, during the summer. By the end of 1944, however, he was squiring Jeanne seriously, and in December, one interested columnist observed the couple was "really vooming." For Christmas, the young star wanted to give her beau a nice gift, but her mother wouldn't allow her to buy him anything more personal than a wallet. She obeyed Loretta, but Paul, with no obligation to reciprocate the limitation, bought Jeanne a beautiful bracelet. Knowing her mother wouldn't permit her keeping the bauble, she hid it.

Paul's career as an actor began in the spring of 1944, when, using the professional name Paul Brooks, he joined fifty-one other featured players under contract to Warner Brothers. Errol Flynn was still one of the studio's top box-office draws, but the unruly actor was constantly at odds with Jack Warner and others in the upper echelons of the company. In an attempt to put Flynn in his place, Warners placed Brinkman, almost a double for its tempestuous star, under contract. Brinkman's primary function was to sit in the Warner Brothers Green Room, where the stars and directors lunched, which subsequently annoyed Flynn. Although Brinkman eventually got to appear before the camera, his major acting was reserved for the Green Room during the lunch hour.

Shortly after he signed with Warners, columnist Cal York explained the situation very succinctly when he wrote:

> "Hollywood is also bored with Flynn and his episodes and maybe Warner Brothers are beginning to be, too, seeing they've signed Paul Brinkman, handsome man-about-town and Flynn's exact double ... Brinkman once squired Lili Damita [Flynn's wife] about when Lili and Flynn were fighting and all the papers reported a reconciliation much to Flynn's rage ...

Warners have changed Brinkman's name to Paul Brooks, so who knows – he may be the next big brave hero of the Flynn epics if Errol doesn't soon quiet down."

Other entertainment writers in Hollywood weren't as enthusiastic and showed sympathy for the novice actor, who was nearly a decade younger than his more famous doppelganger. One observed: "Warner's signing of Paul Brinkman could not be more intriguing. He's the lad who looks like Errol Flynn...Any way you cut it, Brinkman is in a tough spot. People who look like established stars seldom get anywhere." Will McLaughlin noted the studio's new addition with: "Warner Brothers recently signed a young player named Paul Brinkman. Now poor Paul is really in a pickle. He's a dead ringer for Errol Flynn, whose contract is held by the same studio. It wouldn't be so bad if Brinkman had a histrionic reputation of his own on which to fall back. As an unknown, he's definitely on the spot and will have to break his young back to make good."

He made his debut in a small role in *The Doughgirls*, which showcased a large cast headed by A-listers Ann Sheridan and Alexis Smith. It was described by exhibitors as "a very weak picture that few enjoyed." His time at Warners was brief, and his resemblance to Flynn was so strong, he felt "he didn't have a chance there" because of it. Although he appeared in small roles in four pictures, he had secured his release from the studio before *The Doughgirls* hit the screen.

Still not exclusive with Paul, Jeanne went out shortly after the New Year with Henry King, Jr. The couple were dining at Tail O' the Cock, a popular restaurant in Los Angeles, known for its good food and drink instead of its showy atmosphere, when Jeanne saw Paul with another girl just a few tables from hers. Uncomfortable and jealous, she and Paul talked over the phone later that night and agreed to date only one another. Loretta vehemently objected, telling her that she was too young to be so exclusive with Brinkman, encouraging her to date other young men, and reminding her daughter of her promising movie career. She had never defied Loretta, and along with Rita, the three had been inseparable since the Crains' divorce, except for the girls' time with their grandparents. Fox backed Mrs. Crain up, preferring "their little Jeanne wait until she's older" regarding any marriage talk. Feeling pressure from both the studio and her mother, Jeanne appeased Loretta, and in the spring of 1945, she and Paul broke it off.

For four months they didn't see one another, instead going out with other people. During this time Jeanne was on location, shooting *Leave Her to Heaven*, and Paul had signed with RKO Pictures, where his career didn't fare much better than it had at Warner Brothers. His first appearance at the studio was an uncredited role as a pilot in the wartime comedy-romance, *Those Endearing Young Charms*. He then moved on to a series of short comedies with titles like *What, No Cigarettes?*, *Double Honeymoon* and *The Big Beef* (all released in 1945). He also focused on his engineering endeavors, obtaining a patent for a radio receiver that he designed, and starting his own radio manufacturing company.

Their four-month separation made both Jeanne and Paul miserable and on V-J Day they reconciled and eventually made plans to be married. As Christmastime approached, Jeanne made a date with Paul for Christmas Eve. Loretta wasn't happy about the arrangement and wanted her daughter to be home for the holiday. When Jeanne announced that she and Paul were planning to marry, her mother became very upset and she and Jeanne quarreled, resulting in "many stormy scenes and tears." Loretta refused to allow Paul into their house. When he arrived to see Jeanne, he pounded on the door and the distraught young star rushed away with him. Mrs. Crain had insisted that the couple postpone any wedding plans, but from Jeanne's perspective she was just finishing up filming on *Centennial Summer* and about to start her new picture. She knew it might be a long time before she was free and even then, she wasn't sure if her mother would give her consent. When her daughter didn't return, Loretta began looking for her, calling the Brinkman home, where Paul lived with his parents. She wasn't there, nor at any of her friends' homes. Mrs. Crain became very worried.

    Instead of going to the Brinkmans' house, which, despite the presence of the elder Brinkmans, could have produced whispers from evil minds, or the impersonal detachment of a hotel room, Paul took Jeanne to Marshall and Bobby Kester's San Fernando Valley ranch, where the two had originally met. They decided to get married the following Saturday, December 29, at Jeanne's parish church. They had, however, forgotten the strict Catholic requirement of three readings of the banns before marriage. This was a series of announcements of an upcoming wedding among those of the Catholic faith, made over the course of three consecutive Sundays. During the war, there was a dispensation excusing the requirement, but as the war had ended it had been revoked, which meant the couple would have to wait until January 6 to marry. They made an appeal to Bishop

Mr. and Mrs. Paul Brinkman on their wedding day,
December 31, 1945
(Courtesy of the Jeanne Crain Brinkman Family Trust)

McGucken of the Archdiocese of Los Angeles and he granted their plea for a special dispensation, allowing them to be married on December 31. A photographer was at thecourthouse to capture the couple filling out their application for a marriage license the following Friday.

Jeanne stayed with the Kesters all week, having no contact with her mother since their argument. Although she was "terribly worried" about her daughter, Loretta didn't report her as missing to the police, instead letting the Fox publicity department handle the situation.

Finally, on Monday morning, New Year's Eve, Reverend Eugene Ivancovich married the strikingly handsome couple at the Church of the Blessed Sacrament in Hollywood, in front of a handful of guests, none of which were from the bride's family. Jeanne's ensemble was completely white, as it should be, including a simple tailored gabardine suit, halo felt hat, matching pumps and orchids. On her finger was her wedding ring, a design of interwoven orange blossoms studded with diamonds and baguette rubies. The witnesses were Bobby Kester, who had introduced the newlyweds over two years earlier, and W.L. Marxer, the Brinkman's Beverly Hills doctor and son-in-law to silent film star, Francis X. Bushman. In fact, the happy day fell on the second anniversary of their first date. After the nuptials, the couple went to Paul's home, where the groom carried his bride over the threshold for photographers. Jeanne wanted to contact her mother, but a newspaperman had made the call first, a move which hurt Loretta and caused Jeanne to break down in tears.

After a bridal breakfast at the Kester's home, which included members of the wedding party and the groom's parents, the newlyweds posed for studio publicity photos. The couple then drove away in Paul's father's Cadillac. Before heading out to their honeymoon destination of the Furnace Creek Inn, a retreat in the Mojave Desert, Jeanne wanted to stop by her mother's house. She was saddened to find that Loretta wasn't there, having left in an upset state to stay with friends. Their five-day honeymoon in Death Valley included horseback riding and exploring old mine shafts in the desert, but Jeanne confessed that her marriage wasn't completely happy until she returned home and was reconciled with her mother.

{ 6 }
1946 – The Year of Jeanne

The Brinkman's honeymoon ended when Jeanne had to return to Los Angeles to appear in a radio version of *Seventh Heaven* with fellow Fox star Tyrone Power, who was making his first public appearance since being released from the US Marines. The program was the premiere performance of *Hollywood Star Time*, a radio dramatic anthology "featuring big name movie talent and hit films." Being chosen to star in the debut episode of a quality program, which also happened to be superstar Power's first post-war broadcast, was a testament to how popular Crain had become as a celebrity, and how far her career had advanced.

At the same time she was reuniting with Paul, she had been filming *Centennial Summer*, a musical set in Philadelphia during the Centennial Exhibition of 1876. The event was the celebration of the United States' 100th anniversary and was the first official world's fair in the country. The movie centers on the Rogers family, headed by Jesse, a railroad foreman, (Walter Brennan) his wife Harriet, (Dorothy Gish) and their four children, though the two youngest siblings are barely visible with the most screen time going to the older Rogers girls, Julia (Crain) and Edith (Linda Darnell).

Fox had purchased the film rights to the novel by Albert E. Idell as early as September 1943 and initially had no plans to make it into a musical, but in the latter half of 1944, with the success of *Meet Me in St. Louis* at MGM, the transition into that genre began. Famed songwriter Jerome Kern was hired in early 1945 (although he would die later that year before the film was released) and Otto Preminger, with whom Jeanne had worked on *In the Meantime, Darling*, was assigned to direct. It was Crain's first costume picture and when asked by a Hollywood reporter what she thought of her debut historical venture, she confessed it was "not a thing of joy," replying: "It's this corset," she said. "Every time I sit down to eat, I wonder just where the food's going to go. I've been cinched up in this harness every day for the past ten weeks."

Jeanne and Cornel Wilde in *Centennial Summer* (1946)

Off-screen, she and Paul led an idyllic life of wedded bliss. Although he appeared briefly in a few 1946 releases at RKO, including a featured role in *The Falcon's Alibi*, he turned his attention to business, specifically his radio manufacturing concern. As a wedding gift, he presented Jeanne with a bleached mahogany radio, trimmed with pigskin leather. The couple lived in a house loaned to them by Paul's friend, Huntington Hartford, young heir to the A&P supermarket fortune, while they searched for acreage to build their dream home.

Darryl Zanuck continued to look out for Crain's best interest. The young actress had been set to play the title character in Fox's upcoming big budget western, *My Darling Clementine*, directed by John Ford and sporting a top line cast of Fox stars, including Henry Fonda, Victor Mature and Linda Darnell, with whom Jeanne was then filming *Centennial Summer*. Enticing as playing the title character may have sounded, Clementine was a very small role in the film, arguably less than secondary. Jeanne's celebrity had exploded after *State Fair* and in late February 1946, Zanuck sent Ford a memo explaining that it was impossible to cast Crain in such an insignificant part.

> "There will be no chance for us to get Jeanne Crain to play in *My Darling Clementine*. I know she would be delighted to be directed by you but the part is comparatively so small that we would be simply crucified by both the public and the critics by putting her in it. She is the biggest box-office attraction on the lot today. There is no one even second to her...."

The young star's popularity had grown so rapidly that her fan mail had increased to 2,000 letters a week and was second only to Betty Grable, who had been the studio's top star for several years. Instead of *Clementine*, Crain was cast in a picture that would rest solely on her name and star value. In fact, *Life* magazine recognized it as "the first movie which was bound to stand or fall on her performance." As early as January 1945, Jeanne was named as the lead in *Maggie*, an original story written by husband and wife team, Richard Branstan and Ruth McKenny, about a shy, young schoolgirl in late 1920s Ohio. It was planned as a nostalgic musical, shot in Technicolor, and Jeanne's singing would again be dubbed by Louanne Hogan. By the time filming began a year later the title had changed to *Margie* and Crain had become a star with her appearances in *State Fair* and *Leave Her to Heaven*. Her role in *Margie* was so significant, that Cornel Wilde, her costar in *Leave Her to Heaven*, was put on suspension by the studio for refusing to play her romantic interest, a part which the actor deemed "colorless... uninteresting and subordinate to Jeanne Crain." Glenn Langan, a young actor who was being groomed by Fox, was cast instead.

The movie's production manager, Robert Webb, wanted to shoot against a background that looked like a midwestern high school in the late or middle 1920s. With Reno, Nevada in mind for such a spot, he flew over the town, which seemed perfect, especially for the street scenes. He then approached the president of the University of Nevada, located in Reno, about photographing the campus buildings as a high school. He also wisely utilized the university's student population as extras in the film. Webb later recalled how the school term schedule played a role in casting the picture.

"We needed university students to portray our high-school students, because it would have made our stars, Jeanne Crain and Conrad Janis, and others of the cast who are older than high school age, look like hags and old gaffers if we had put high school students alongside them. Also, we had to find out if we could get college students out of school in time each day to work for us. The holiday between semesters solved that problem. The semester end was just around the corner."

About three hundred UN students were hired as extras for $7.50 a day. Additional students were hired to haul snow down from Mount Rose to give Reno a wintry look. Social security applications were made available to those who had no card and the company advertised for locals to bring any bicycles or cars made prior to 1929 for use in the film. The crew spent the first days of shooting on location, photographing snow scenes on campus. The temperature was four degrees above zero, which caused several problems. The sound recording machines showed signs of freezing and the young people, bundled in furs, galoshes and long flannel underwear, found it difficult to perform their dance routines.

When the troupe returned to Hollywood to prepare for work on the sound stages, delays continued because some of the youngsters had colds and needed a few days of rest. Therefore, the Call Sheet for Friday summoned only Esther Dale, who played the grandmother, and Hobart Cavanaugh, Margie's father. Veteran character actress Hattie McDaniel filmed an outdoor scene, hanging clothes in the backyard, with the thermometer not much above zero. To stay warm in between takes, McDaniel sat in a car with a local driver, who enjoyed the crisp, mountain air. "Isn't this wonderful weather," he proclaimed. "Nothing like it. Wonderful weather," to which McDaniel would respond, "Yes, wonderful weather. If you don't have to get out in it."

Alan Young, a radio comedian, was cast as Roy Hornsdale, Margie's awkward, poetry-spouting beau. It was Young's film debut and he would later recount those early days on the set with his lovely costar and her new husband.

> [Jeanne] spent her honeymoon making *Margie*! Her husband, Paul Brinkman, was with us on location, which our director, Henry King, thought was a bit of a distraction, but he stayed around. [She] was very much like she was in the picture — wide-eyed but very intelligent, maybe a little sharper than she appeared. And she was so beautiful: you could dip a spoon into her skin like ice cream.

Indeed, when the company went on location to Reno, Jeanne and Paul had been married only a few weeks, and Jeanne was asked to ride up with the other members of the company in the studio car. The newlywed, usually very cooperative, rebelled at the request and announced that her husband would drive her up in his convertible. When the Fox crew reached Reno, they kept their eyes open for Jeanne and Paul. After a few hours with no sign of the couple, studio officials began to phone the towns through which they might have passed. Six hours later they arrived, greeted by the worried group. They had taken a leisurely route different from the one followed by the studio convoy. While Jeanne was working on the set, Paul would go skiing at a neighboring resort and on her afternoons off, the couple would go skiing together at nearby Mount Rose, even making the pages of the local newspaper in their sporting gear.

Some newspaper columns in Los Angeles began carrying items to the effect that Brinkman hung around Jeanne's set all day, offering advice on acting. When Crain was still slated for a role in *My Darling Clementine*, director John Ford had made arrangements for location work to be done in New Mexico and Arizona. One newspaper item noted that "if Paul Brinkman continues going on locations with his bride... he's going to be a much-traveled young man." Defending her husband, Jeanne explained: "The actual truth was that I was just beginning to learn how to drive then, so Paul drove me to the studio each morning and called for me on the way home, just as my mother had done before I was married. At the time, I had to have someone drive me. Paul never remained on the sets — he was much too busy, and he never gave me any advice about acting, even when I asked for it." Nonetheless, the "too frequent visits" Paul paid to the set were starting to get "into Twentieth Century-Fox's hair." The studio had been wary about Jeanne's marriage to Brinkman from the beginning and now its top brass was getting annoyed with his interference in his wife's career. Shortly after these stories made their rounds, Jeanne bought a car and Paul taught her how to drive, so she could transport herself to the studio daily and her husband could "stay home and out of range of the gossips."

Tensions between Jeanne and her mother had eased but Loretta was still unconvinced that the marriage was best for her daughter. The trip to Reno for location shooting of *Margie* was the first time such travel didn't include Loretta and Rita. During the filming, Jeanne wrote her mother,

Signing autographs for fans on the *Margie* set in Reno, Nevada, 1946

while on the set, telling her how much she enjoyed the shoot:

> "All day today we reshot the first day's work because Mr. King [director Henry King] wanted to use the snow. I am glad because it is much prettier. He is so nice. We have talked to him a lot and have lunch with him nearly every day. I am having a lot of fun in this role - I look very funny but the funnier the better for the picture."

The Reno filming experience was a pleasant one for Jeanne, and she interacted with all strata of university social levels. In her *Margie* wardrobe, she signed autographs for students on campus, and early in the shooting schedule, she and director King were the honored guests of the university's president, Dr. John Moseley, at a dinner party, attended by the governor of Nevada. Crain would later remember the campus as a friendly, easy place to be. "It was like a family," she said. "Everyone knew each other."

While *Margie* was in post-production, *Centennial Summer* was released. Accompanied by her new husband, Jeanne attended the world premiere in Philadelphia, along with director Preminger, in early July. The three-day event was a "publicity agent's dream," with the same pomp and circumstance that had accorded *Home in Indiana* and *State Fair*, including a reception at City Hall for Crain and the delegation of Twentieth Century-Fox players who accompanied her. She then rode in a parade to the Bellevue-Stratford Hotel, where she and the others were guests at an official luncheon, hosted by the mayor and attended by legislators, as well as civic and industry executives. That evening the stars were driven to the Fox Theater by police escort, where huge crowds waited their arrival. The Philadelphia festivities were the kick-off to other premieres which were set across the country.

The movie's reception was lukewarm and the reviews for both the film and its stars were less than stellar. Bosley Crowther of the *New York Times* observed it "limps along heavily and slowly [and] Jeanne Crain and Linda Darnell are elaborately artificial and woefully deficient as to voice." If his analysis was accurate, it failed to take into account that both actresses had been dubbed in their singing. Despite the lackluster response to *Centennial Summer*, Fox renewed Crain's contract under new terms and named her as star in several potential films. *Party Line, Chicken Every Sunday* and *No Wedding Ring* were three projects with her name announced as the lead performer, the latter originally given to Betty Grable.

Unlike *Centennial Summer*, *Margie* was a bona fide hit. In September, *Life* magazine celebrated the highly anticipated movie with a cover shot of Jeanne in a bubble bath, one of the scenes from the picture. The movie had its New York premiere at the Roxy Theatre on October 16, the same day *My Darling Clementine* made its debut in San Francisco. With *Margie*, the Roxy saw its biggest non-holiday week gross in twenty years, and it set pre-release box-office records all over the country. The film made its western premiere at the Majestic Theatre in Reno at the end of October, with Barbara Lawrence (who played Margie's best-friend/rival, Marybelle Tenor) and Glen Langan in attendance.

In contrast to her mixed notices for *Centennial Summer*, movie reviewers were in pleasant accord about Jeanne's performance in *Margie*, giving her the thumbs-up attention of a star who had arrived. *Box Office Digest* proclaimed, "Jeanne Crain meets exacting demands with hitherto histrionic skill," while the *New York Post* said, "Jeanne Crain is the essence of adolescent appeal... Margie is a real gem." When the year ended, she had starred in the top two highest grossing films at Twentieth Century-Fox for 1946: *Leave Her to Heaven* and *Margie*, the latter grossing over $4 million and standing on her name value alone. The success of *Margie* was not lost on Zanuck. He was so pleased with the box-office receipts and public response that he started planning a semi-sequel, set in the Roaring '20s, to be called

The Flapper. He hoped to use Jeanne again, as it was her performance that contributed so much to the success of the earlier picture, but her filming schedule had been postponed for the near future. Despite having several hit movies under her belt, nature had halted her ascending career. She was expecting a baby.

{ 7 }
Motherhood and Addie Ross

After Jeanne discovered she was pregnant, she hoped to be able to make one more picture before the child was born in the spring of 1947. She denied that she was expecting until columnist Sheilah Graham proclaimed that "it is obvious she is approaching motherhood." Even before Jeanne realized she was pregnant, she and Paul had continued searching for the perfect spot to build their home. Upon the suggestion of Huntington Hartford, they looked at acreage in Outpost Estates, an exclusive hillside development in the western hills of Hollywood, where the red tiled roofs and plentiful patios of Spanish and Mediterranean style homes populated the landscape. The property was high on a hill where scenic stretches of Los Angeles, Hollywood, Beverly Hills and the San Fernando Valley could be viewed with ease. They acquired the land and began working with Walter Wurdeman, a noted architect who designed the Pan-Pacific Auditorium, the entity which teenaged Crain had represented as a beauty pageant winner. Their envisioned structure would include a wall made entirely of glass, with a fireplace built in, to be able to enjoy both a cozy fire as well as the fantastic California view.

By spring 1946, Jeanne and Paul had found an apartment in Santa Monica to live in until their dream home was built. Shortly after they moved into their new place, they attended a Hollywood circus party hosted by noted radio manufacturing millionaire Atwater Kent, at his Bel-Air mansion. A lavish affair, it featured a menagerie of exotic animals such as elephants, camels and seals. In a miniature cage was a cute, ten-day old lion cub, which was taken out only to have cigarette smoke blown in its face and be otherwise teased by the guests. Feeling sorry for the animal and to save it from any further mishandling, the Brinkmans adopted it as their pet and smuggled it into their newly acquired apartment. They named the baby lioness Shah-Shah and the unorthodox roommate became the subject of newspaper headlines throughout her time with the couple. After Shah-Shah escaped from the apartment and was hit by a car, Jeanne began taking her along on evenings out with Paul, causing much consternation wherever they ended up.

Jeanne with lion cub, Shah-Shah, 1946
(Courtesy of the Jeanne Crain Brinkman Family Trust)

Although she took a hiatus from her career, it didn't affect her standing at Fox. If anything, she entered her maternity leave with high anticipation from the studio about her return. *Margie* had been the peak of her short tenure and things only looked to go up from there. In early February, her contract was extended, and although her baby wasn't expected for a couple more months, she was announced to star in a remake of *Ramona*, a much-filmed story that Crain had longed to play. The movie never materialized but others were in the works for her, though some, like *Chicken Every Sunday*, would be made with other stars due to her pregnancy.

Early expectations had her baby due around St. Patrick's Day, 1947, but when that date passed, she hoped for the child to be born on Paul's birthday, which was April 10. On the Saturday before Easter, the Brinkmans went out to dinner and a movie. By the time they got back to their apartment Jeanne's pains were regular and Paul took her to the Queen of Angels Hospital, the premier medical facility in Southern California. They entered the hospital at 12:30 on Easter morning and by 5:15 a.m. a baby boy was delivered by Dr. Alphonsus McCarthy, who had overseen the birth of three other babies that night. They named their son after his father, and shortly after his birth, the small family, including Shah-Shah, moved into their new house on Outpost Cove Drive, a modern, ranch-style structure with all the amenities. The plate-glassed walls were in place, just as they had hoped, as well as a rough pine ceiling, which was stained green. The glassed wall extended into the couple's bedroom, which looked out over their bean-shaped swimming pool, an addition afforded due to Paul's decision to be his own contractor.

As Shah-Shah's first birthday came and went, the cute cub had grown into a muscular, 200 lb. lion. The Brinkmans' Hollywood Hills neighbors were not amused at the animal's loud roar and were unnerved when she kicked in the wall of a large dog house, even though she was kept behind a wire fence on the property. Complaints began coming in to the office of the Chief Deputy City Attorney Boyd Taylor, who dispatched two officers to the Brinkmans' hilltop estate with a summons to appear before him with their plans regarding the lion's future, as well as citing Crain for keeping the animal without a license. Forced to make arrangements for their pet to live in a more appropriate place, Jeanne and Paul reluctantly donated Shah-Shah to the Griffith Park Zoo.

With Shah-Shah no longer an issue, the Brinkmans planned a vacation before Jeanne had to report back to the studio to start her new picture, *The Flapper*, which had now been renamed *The Flaming Age*. The week after the lioness was released to the zoo, however, Jeanne's mother, Loretta, was seriously ill after undergoing an operation. Jeanne canceled the trip and when her mother suffered a relapse in late September, she stayed with her constantly.

After an eighteen-month maternity leave, Jeanne returned to the studio. By the end of 1947, Betty Grable was still firmly entrenched as the queen at Twentieth Century-Fox, but even accounting for her time away, Crain was "running Grable a close second," with several movies waiting in the wings. After *The Flaming Age* (which had changed titles yet again, this time to *You Were Meant for Me*), she had been named for starring roles in *Apartment for Susie, Julie, Mr. Cooper's Left Hand* and she was at the time still in contention for the lead in *Chicken Every Sunday*. All but

Paul, Jeanne and Shah-Shah, 1947
(Courtesy of the Jeanne Crain Brinkman Family Trust)

You Were Meant for Me and *Apartment for Susie* would go to other actresses, but just the volume of interest by producers at Fox to use the young star secured her place at the studio.

Producers at her own studio weren't the only ones clamoring for her services upon her return to the screen. Charles Feldman, a leading Hollywood talent agent who was transitioning to producing, wanted to use her in his upcoming prestige project, *The Glass Menagerie*, based on the successful Broadway play by Tennessee Williams. Feldman planned to cast Crain as the fragile Laura, along with Ethel Barrymore as her mother, Amanda. Although one movie trade publication called it the "most important role of her [Crain] career," neither Jeanne nor Barrymore were used when the film made it to the screen with Jane Wyman and Gertrude Lawrence, hired respectively, in 1950. Also, Orson Welles, who unsuccessfully tested Jeanne when she was a teenager, a half a decade before, asked Twentieth Century-Fox to loan her out to play Roxanne in his production of *Cyrano de Bergerac*. The young star was riding a huge wave of success.

Instead of straying from the fold, Crain jumped into *You Were Meant for Me*, with song-and-dance man, Dan Dailey. The film was Zanuck's attempt to capitalize on the success of *Margie* and Dailey's *Mother Wore Tights*, which were both period musicals. It was a semi-remake of the studio's 1942 hit, *Orchestra Wives*, and featured Jeanne as Peggy Mayhugh, a pretty, eighteen-year-old who meets orchestra leader Chuck Arnold (Dailey), when his band, The Sophisticates, plays in her small Indiana town. After a whirlwind courtship, Peggy and Chuck marry, but the new bride finds life on the road with a swing band more difficult than she expected. The couple endures many marital trials, including the stock market crash of 1929 and the breakup of the band, but at the final fade-out, per the happy endings of such pictures, all is well. *You Were Meant for Me* was released in February 1948. It wasn't the hit that *Margie* had been, but it held its own, landing in the top seventy-five box-office winners for the year. Of Jeanne's performance, the *Showmen's Trade Review* wrote she "is capable, charming and a joy to watch."

In February 1948, Crain found herself once again in Reno, Nevada for location filming on her next picture, *Apartment for Jenny*. It was based on a novelette of the

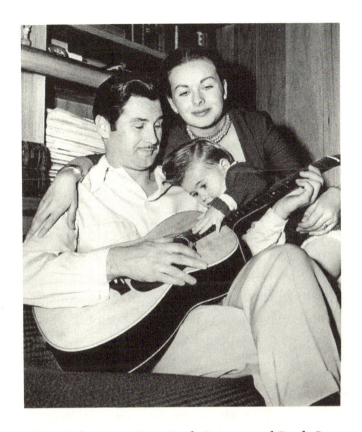

The Brinkmans, 1947, Paul, Jeanne and Paul, Jr.
(Courtesy of the Jeanne Crain Brinkman Family Trust)

same name by Faith Baldwin, a prolific writer of popular fiction. Another film being produced at the same time was *Portrait of Jennie*, starring Jennifer Jones, and to differentiate the two, Fox changed the title of its picture to *Apartment for Susie*. Initially, the film's leading male character was to be played by Richard Widmark, an actor who made his film debut just months earlier in *Kiss of Death*, a chilling film noir starring Victor Mature. The role of a good-natured G.I. in a Jeanne Crain picture was a far cry from his turn as a giggling, menacing sociopath in the earlier movie. Instead, Fox borrowed William Holden from Paramount for the part and made one final title change: *Apartment for Peggy*.

Baldwin's story was adapted as a comedy-drama about a depressed college professor named Henry Barnes who is determined to commit suicide. He then meets Peggy Taylor, an energetic and enthusiastic young woman whose husband, Jason, is a Navy veteran, attending college on the G.I. Bill. Peggy is pregnant and in dire need of better lodging, since she and Jason currently reside in a cramped camper on campus. She persuades the professor to rent out his attic, bringing brightness and a sense of belonging to his lonely, melancholy existence. The movie explores both the college experience of many post-war servicemen seeking to improve their lot in life, as well as the potential emptiness of old-age.

Edmund Gwenn, who played Professor Barnes, had found star status the previous year, when he won an Academy Award for playing Kris Kringle in *Miracle on 34th Street*. In *Apartment for Peggy*, he shared top-billing with Crain and William Holden and more than held his own with his younger, higher-profile costars. Before he signed on for the part of Jason Taylor, William Holden requested of the film's director, George Seaton, that the screenplay be rewritten to make his role more prominent. Seaton explained that he felt the script had just the right balance as it was, but offered to add anything extra to the part if (and only if) it helped to better the story. Holden shook Seaton's hand, exclaiming, "At least you're honest. Okay, you've got me."

The trio of stars got along well on the set, though each had their own, very different acting techniques. Director Seaton revealed later that Jeanne "had very slow delivery of her lines," something that did not work well with comedy, so he wrote her character "as someone who had diarrhea of the mouth." She had to talk very fast and energetically, which became part of her characterization and helped her refrain from the deliberate delivery she was used to. Seaton's guidance helped attract critical acclaim for Jeanne's performance, when the movie premiered in October. Bosley Crowther, of the *New York Times*, wrote enthusiastically of both youthful leads: "It is the true demonstration of a GI student, which William Holden plays, and, especially, the vivid characterization, by Jeanne Crain, of his wife." *Variety* also sang her praises, proclaiming: "Jeanne Crain is perfect casting for the young wife..." Upon its general release, *Apartment for Peggy* was a box-office hit and it became one of the top grossing films of 1948.

Besides getting plum roles in high-profile movies when she returned to Fox, Jeanne's career got another boost from the Academy of Motion Picture Arts and Sciences, when they admitted her to membership along with sixteen other actors, including Alexis Smith, Shelley Winters and fellow Fox player, Anne Baxter. Crain and Baxter were also slated to costar in Jeanne's next picture, *A Letter to Four Wives*. The upcoming film started out as a story in *Cosmopolitan* magazine called "One of Our Hearts," which was expanded into a novel by its author, John Klempner, and retitled, *A Letter to Five Wives*. The novelization was featured in the August 1945 issue of *Cosmo*, and Fox became interested in it as a potential movie in 1946, purchasing the film rights the same year. Vera Caspary, the author of the novel, *Laura*, on which the movie of the same named was based, wrote a screen treatment, and screenwriter and director Joseph L. Mankiewicz had a screenplay penned by the end of April, 1948. By the time it reached Zanuck's hands, the *Wives* had been pared down to four, with Jeanne, Baxter, Linda Darnell and Ann Sothern, borrowed from MGM, cast to play them. Zanuck "liked the script immensely" and though it was "beautifully written," he thought four storylines were still too many, and felt the segment on Martha and Roger (featuring Baxter) was "dull." Consequently, he told Mankiewicz to cut out one of the couples from the script. Baxter was out, and Mankiewicz would later admit that the elimination of one of the couples produced a better picture.

The story is set in American suburbia circa 1948 ("just 28 minutes from the big city, 23 if you catch the morning express") and it revolves around three upper-middle class wives (actually one is striving to be upper middle class). Just as they're boarding a boat, to act as chaperones of a day-long children's charity picnic, they receive a letter (one letter addressed to all three) from their "friend," who is also the town flirt, saying she has run off with one of their husbands, but doesn't say which one. Caught between shock, disbelief and nagging suspicion, they board the boat and begin a journey that not only takes them up river but through the emotional status of their respective marriages. Each reflects, via flashback, on the weaknesses in her union, and dwells on the fact that her husband was very friendly with the vampish letter writer, named Addie Ross, at some point in his life.

Mankiewicz traveled to the East coast to scope out locations for shooting which would reflect both suburban Northeast America, as well as outdoor recreational areas along the Hudson River. Lake Mahopac, a resort about fifty miles from New York City, and Stamford, Connecticut were chosen and crews were sent to these locations in early June to start shooting. Jeanne and her fellow "wives" also made their way to New York State, where signs of a feud were reported between Linda Darnell and Ann Sothern. Darnell and Crain, who had worked amiably together in *Centennial Summer*, got along very well, however. Linda even accompanied Jeanne to New York City one evening while on location to meet Paul for dinner at the Stork Club.

A Letter to Three Wives (1949), with Linda Darnell, Ann Sothern and Jeanne

Although she was top-billed, the segment featuring Jeanne and Jeffrey Lynn, who played her character's husband, was by far the weakest of the three. Still engaging, capturing its characterizations through scintillating dialogue and great performances, the Crain-Lynn segment doesn't have the cutting wit provided by the other wives' slice of celluloid. Mankiewicz, whose first film this was to both write and direct, was neither encouraged by Jeanne's performance, nor her method of acting. He would later vent to Zanuck how displeased he was, saying:

> "I had to overcome the entire opening scene because this Crain girl cannot project anything. She doesn't want to be an actress. She's a very sweet woman, who, at the end of the day, hangs her performance on a vaudeville hook and goes home to her husband Paul Brinkman, who happened to be a very nice man. And she was a very nice girl, but she didn't *live* being an actress."

He had not always, however, been so disenchanted with the young star's abilities. In 1946, he had requested, more than once, that Zanuck allow him to cast her as Agnes in his prestige production, *The Late George Apley*, which starred Ronald Colman. The movie was, nonetheless, a major success, both with critics and audiences, and garnered Oscars for Mankiewicz in both the screenwriting and directing categories.

Just before production began on *A Letter to Three Wives*, Jeanne was told that she would have the lead role and top-billing (which had become the norm for her pictures) in an upcoming project called *The Fan*, based on Oscar Wilde's Victorian-era play, *Lady Windermere's Fan*. The part of young and beautiful Lady Windermere was originally given to studio glamour-girl Gene Tierney. The sultry star had to be replaced, however, when she announced that she was pregnant, or, as one columnist put it so sprightly, "Gene bowed out because of approaching motherhood and the little

Crain girl stepped in gladly." The "little Crain girl" was actually riding a wave of enormous success and Tierney wouldn't see another major box-office hit during her career. One reporter put it less delicately by pointing out that Jeanne, "doing the sweet-little-girl jobs in Zanuck-land, has just gently plopped Gene Tierney down from her satin seat on top of the Fox lady-star heap."

In reality, Jeanne was "approaching motherhood" again herself, though not nearly as far along in her pregnancy as Tierney. She wanted to work as long as she could before taking maternity leave, so she began work on *The Fan* immediately after *A Letter to Three Wives*. Production began in early July, and Jeanne worked for the third time with director Otto Preminger, to whom she did not confide her current condition. Her cause for making the picture as quickly as possible was helped when Preminger was able to start the project a week earlier than anticipated, due to the sooner than expected availability of costar, Richard Greene. Her condition only showed itself one hot day on the set when she fainted, while cinched within an old-fashioned, whale-boned corset, the stylish undergarment of Victorian England.

As the top-billed star of *The Fan*, Crain didn't show up on screen until eighteen minutes into the movie. Instead, film veteran Madeline Carroll makes the first appearance and impression as Mrs. Erlynne, the mysterious middle-aged beauty who unintentionally wreaks havoc in the marriage of Lord and Lady Windermere in 1890s London. Jeanne was beautiful and elegantly graceful as the young, conservative-minded Margaret Windermere. Carroll and fellow Brit George Sanders overshadowed the less experienced Crain and Greene, however, and much of Oscar Wilde's biting wit was missing. When *The Fan* was released the following spring, reviews of Jeanne's performance were mixed, with Bosley Crowther of the *New York Times* proclaiming, "Jeanne Crain is perforce insipid, being made by direction to appear quite dull." *Variety*, however, took a completely opposite view, writing, "Miss Crain, as Lady Windermere, achieves further acting laurels in what is perhaps her best screen role to date."

When she completed work on *The Fan*, Jeanne didn't begin another picture, instead taking maternity time to await the birth of her second child. The expectant mother was hoping for a girl this time, and had already picked out the name Diane Jeanne, but, on January 21, 1949, at the Queen of Angels Hospital, a second son was born to the Brinkmans, weighing in at seven pounds, twelve ounces. The boy was named Michael Anthony, and joined his brother, Paul, Jr., in mugging for the publicity camera within weeks of his birth. With her career in high gear, Jeanne was anxious to get back to work after Michael was born. She was already making tests for an upcoming picture less than a month after giving birth. She wanted to be part of an exciting, groundbreaking project being planned at Fox, a movie which could be her most dramatic and important to date. It was called *Pinky*.

{ 8 }
Pinky

After the war ended, the motion picture industry was ready to tackle social topics that hadn't seen much screen time in the past. Darryl Zanuck was at the head of the pack, and in 1947 he took on antisemitism, winning a Best Picture Oscar with a pet project called *Gentleman's Agreement*. He followed it in 1948 with another success, *The Snake Pit*, delving into the subject of mental illness. By 1949 he was ready to produce another "message" picture and this time it would address racial injustice.

Having risen in the ranks as both producer and director at Fox after his success with *Laura*, Otto Preminger was, in his own words, "as autonomous as any producer, any director, at that time could be." His influence, however, was within the confines of the Fox system, and any potential movie project had to be approved by the boss. He was, therefore, always on the lookout for good film prospects, and in the post-war era, particularly those social dramas that interested Zanuck. He read a book called *Quality*, by Mississippi-born author Cid Ricketts Sumner. It was published in 1946 and told the story of a young, educated African-American woman, who returns to her Southern home, after passing as white in the North, where she attended nursing school. It was selected as a Negro Book Choice, and a *Book Week* reviewer proclaimed: "Mrs. Sumner, white, and born in the South, has written a book of genuine human insight and social perception. I hope it becomes a bestseller."

(l.) *Quality*, by Cid Ricketts Sumner, the novel on which *Pinky* was based. (r.) Jeanne with Ethel Waters in *Pinky* (1949)

Seeing it as the kind of story Zanuck was looking for, Preminger brought the book to his attention, with the hopes of being able to make it as a movie. Zanuck was indeed interested enough to purchase the film rights, and when Preminger asked him about heading the production, he was told by the mogul, "No, I want to produce this myself with John Ford as director." Preminger was dismayed and when he complained he was told that Zanuck simply shrugged his shoulders and replied: "What would a Kraut know about such things, anyway." Disappointed as he was, Preminger later acknowledged: "These things are inevitable because Zanuck ran the studio, and he ran it his way, and I as a grown-up person had to recognize this. I had a contract, got paid, and did the things I wanted to do within the limitations they imposed on us." As he had illustrated to Preminger, Zanuck took on the project as his personal production, and Ford was signed to direct, by way of an outside picture deal with Fox in January 1949. Ford was seen as a good choice for the film because, unlike many of his directing peers in Hollywood, he had used African-American characters in his films, while also treating them sympathetically. Also, he owed Zanuck a film for allowing him to use contract player, Henry Fonda, in Ford's feature, *The Fugitive*.

Screenwriters Philip Dunne and Dudley Nichols had been working on a script for the film since the autumn of 1948, presenting different angles to the racial issues involved and changing the title of the film to *Pinky*. Zanuck, however, was very clear in what he wanted the screenplay to reflect. In an interoffice memo to Nichols he wrote:

> "The reason I have vacillated so much about *Pinky* is because in my heart I am certain that at this point it is not a good enough movie... I am writing in large letters on my script the following legend:
>
> THIS IS NOT A STORY ABOUT HOW TO SOLVE THE NEGRO PROBLEM IN THE SOUTH OR ANYWHERE ELSE. THIS IS NOT A STORY PARTICULARLY ABOUT RACE PROBLEMS, SEGREGATION OR DISCRIMINATION. THIS IS A STORY ABOUT ONE PARTICULAR NEGRO GIRL WHO COULD EASILY PASS AS A WHITE AND WHO DID PASS FOR A WHILE. THIS IS THE STORY OF HOW AND WHY SHE, AS AN INDIVIDUAL, FINALLY DECIDED TO BE HERSELF – A NEGRESS...

In so doing, he centered the story and emotional conflict around the young heroine, Patricia "Pinky" Johnson, a light-skinned African-American nurse, who, after "passing" for white up North, revisits her Southern roots. She is greeted by her grandmother, known to all in the community as Aunt Dicey, but to Pinky she is Granny. Aunt Dicey is an old washerwoman, who works long days taking in other people's laundry to help support her granddaughter in her adopted Northern home. Pinky is also greeted by the poverty she left behind as a teenager, as well as threats and indignation from both the white and black community. As the story unfolds, it is learned that Pinky's return is caused by the emotional confusion she experienced from falling in love with a white, Northern doctor. While in her hometown, she uses her nursing skills to care for an elderly, ornery, aristocratic Southern woman named Miss Em, for whom she at first feels contempt, which gradually changes to respect.

Show business *grande dames* Ethel Barrymore and Ethel Waters were cast as Miss Em and Aunt Dicey, respectively. Several actresses, both black and white, were interested in the role of Pinky. The studio's own contract star, dark and sultry Linda Darnell, wanted to play the part, and African-American singer/actress Lena Horne pleaded with executives at MGM, where she was under contract, to recommend her for the part. As unlikely as it might seem that she be cast, Jeanne wanted the role as well. A week before Michael's birth, she wrote to Zanuck and asked that he consider her. Two weeks after her baby was born, she made a test. In February, she was tentatively named for the lead. Many questioned Zanuck's decision to cast the whitest girl on the lot, and one whose past roles, popular as they might be, were lighthearted fare. Crain's current box-office value was undeniably a boon to her being selected, but there was also the idea that her "whiteness" and pristine screen reputation made Pinky's struggles that much more abhorrent. According to one motion picture commentator, when Ethel Waters' Aunt Dicey makes her living doing laundry the hard way, over boiling cauldrons and under long outdoor drying lines, audiences were neither surprised nor outraged. But when Jeanne Crain was forced to the backbreaking work of using a scrubbing board, with "carefully placed studio sweat rolling off her perfect porcelain-white face," sympathy and shock would be displayed by white audiences.

Production began in mid-March 1949, and there was strife from the outset, specifically surrounding director Ford. He wanted to shoot the film on location in the South, which he felt was crucial to the atmosphere the story needed to convey. Zanuck refused his request, insisting the picture be shot on set at the studio. There was also conflict between Ford and Ethel Waters, who "was frightened to death working for him" and "almost had a stroke." The actress claimed Ford "used the shock treatment" when directing her, though it didn't work well on her as it had on other performers he had browbeaten in the past. His interpretation of her character was a far cry from how she wanted to play the role. Zanuck later recalled how tensions became high during the first week of filming:

> "It was a professional difference of opinion. Ford's Negroes were like Aunt Jemima. Caricatures. I thought we're going to get into trouble. Jack [Ford] said, I think you better put someone else on it. I said, finish out the day, and I took Ford off the

picture. Some directors are great in one field and totally helpless in another field.

On March 17, production was closed down on the movie, due to a back injury suffered by Ford on the set. He tried directing on crutches but was ordered home by his doctor for rest. Filming resumed shortly after. He then developed a case of the shingles, and Zanuck, true to his word, called in Elia Kazan, who had directed *Gentleman's Agreement* for Fox two years earlier, from New York to replace the ailing Ford. It was estimated that the two-week shooting delay, caused by Ford's illness, cost the studio $200,000. According to Kazan, Ford was the American director he "most admired" and he felt it an honor to take his place. The new director, with Zanuck's approval, decided to scrap the Ford footage already shot and start from scratch. After talking with the film's crew, Kazan went to see Zanuck and inquired about the issues that had surfaced before his arrival on the picture. "Jack's not sick," he said, "is he?" Darryl Zanuck answered blatantly, "He just wanted out. He hated that old nigger woman" – meaning Ethel Waters – "and she sure as hell hated him. He scared her next to death." According to Kazan, Ford didn't know how to handle Waters. He couldn't cuss her out, as he had John Wayne, and when he didn't like the way she played a scene, she reacted not with fear "but resentment and retreat."

Kazan eventually found his footing with Waters. It was Jeanne that he had issue with. Like Mankiewicz before him, he found her passive style of acting not to his liking. In his autobiography, the director doesn't even call Crain by name, referring to her as his "leading lady," when commenting on what he perceived as her lack of acting ability. He pulled no punches in his description of directing her in *Pinky*:

> "She was a good soul, a pretty girl, obedient, gentle, yielding, and, I suspected, catechism schooled. She defined the word "ingénue," yet had four children, was to have two more – conceived I wasn't sure how, for she gave the impression of being forever fifteen and intact... Perhaps it was not Ethel but this actress with her goodness who'd brought on Jack's "shingles." There'd be days when I'd long for a bitch!

How well he knew the actress personally is questionable, as his recollection of her children was off by two. He would later call Crain "the blandest person I ever worked with." However, if he found no friend in his leading lady, he enjoyed working with Ethel Barrymore, his self-proclaimed favorite among the cast. During filming, the veteran actress watched Kazan direct Jeanne in several scenes. He said at the end of each take, "That was perfect. Now let's do one more." When he said the same to Miss Barrymore, she turned a quizzical eye on him. "What's the next one for?" she asked, "Your collection?"

Pinky was only one of several "message" films dealing with race being made within months of each other. With screen time being filled with *Intruder in the Dust*, *Home of the Brave*, the independent *Lost Boundaries*, as well as *Pinky*, *Variety* made the observation, "1949 is definitely lining up as the year of the Negro problem pic." Fox would offer up *No Way Out* the following year as well, but of Zanuck's *Pinky*, observers commented on the producers "excellent casting, effective use of natural settings and noble purpose." Being a sensitive social issue for the time, the interracial romance theme was closely monitored by the Production Code Administration in Hollywood. The head of the organization, Joseph Breen, eventually approved the script but in a letter to Fox, he made it clear that "(f)rom the standpoint of general good and welfare, we strongly urge that you avoid physical contact between Negroes and whites, throughout this picture. This, with the idea of avoiding audience offense in a number of sections of this country." The studio explained there would be physical contact in some scenes, but also pointing out that Pinky would be played by a white actress. The production also got input from another front, when Zanuck consulted with Walter White, secretary of the NAACP (National Association for the Advancement of Colored People). White's daughter, Jane White, served as a technical advisor for the picture but discontinued her services when most of her recommendations were ignored.

Jeanne recognized her opportunity to head a quality dramatic film and prepared for the role by reading a book about "passing" and asking introspectively, "how a young Negro girl would feel most every day." Putting herself in Pinky's shoes, she recalled "those times in school when I was humiliated horribly." With Kazan's help to find her motivation, she attempted to convey Pinky's plight to those who felt she was stepping into dangerous social territory. She confided: "So many people have told me not to stir anything up that I feel we've got to really move them into feeling for Pinky and her problems."

After its premiere at New York's Rivoli on September 29, 1949, *Pinky* was an immediate success, though it, unsurprisingly, found criticism from both white and black outlets. Upon its Atlanta opening, there was a police alert in front of the Roxy Theater, but anticipated demonstrations failed to materialize. A local policeman reported "nothing louder than a sneeze" except for one burst of applause in the Negro balcony when Pinky bested an opponent. On the flip side, in Marshall, Texas, a new censorship board was formed in order to prevent a theater from showing the movie. When the theater owner refused to cancel the film, he was imprisoned and fined." Publicity for the film was at a fever pitch, and Crain found herself on the cover of *Life* magazine for a second time.

Jeanne's performance, though not without its critics, was viewed as a dramatic triumph as well, and her growth as an actress of stature noted. One reviewer proclaimed that "Jeanne Crain, as the heroine, does exceptionally fine work," while another went even further, saying she "gives the best performance of her career as Pinky." When ticket sales were tallied at year's end, *Pinky* emerged as Fox's top-grossing film for 1949, bringing in $4.2 million ($42 million in 2017 dollars) and when Academy Award nominations were announced in February 1950, Jeanne's name was among those nominated for Best Actress. Both Ethel Waters and Barrymore were nominated in the Best Supporting Actress category. Although she lost to Olivia de Havilland (in Paramount's *The Heiress*), Crain had broken through her ingénue image (temporarily) and claimed her spot as a dramatic Hollywood actress.

She had come a long way since her one-line debut in a bathing suit, six years earlier. "After all, it's time I grew up," she pointed out to an interviewer. "I had to some time, you know. Everything that's happened in the last three years has been a part of this growing up. I've been married, had two babies and we've planned and built a house. And, hand in hand, along with all that has gone the very, very important part of my life – my work." As the new decade emerged, and Jeanne had her name in the Academy Award hat, she was riding a wave of success, both personally and professionally, and Darryl Zanuck was ready to give his young favorite yet another career break.

{ 9 }
Teen Angst at 25

In the early months of 1950, due to the financial success of *Pinky*, along with monies made from ticket sales for *The Fan* and *A Letter to Three Wives*, *Variety* named Jeanne the number one box-office star of 1949. This huge accomplishment, along with her Oscar nomination and recognition at Grauman's Chinese Theater after *Pinky's* release, made Crain one of the top names in Hollywood, with the new decade open to bright career possibilities for her. Only twenty-four during the early months of the year, Zanuck signed her to a new four-year contract, committing her to forty weeks of work per year.

However, her next scheduled film was a throwback to the roles which had originally brought her to the attention of Hollywood and audiences across America. She was cast as Ann, the eldest daughter in the large Gilbreth brood in the studio's family-oriented production, *Cheaper by the Dozen*. Granted, she was slated for the part before *Pinky* was released, and its reception still unknown, but Jeanne was disappointed, nonetheless, hoping to leave the "girl-next-door" roles behind her and use the momentum created by her role in *Pinky* to play better, more dramatic characters. "After having the best dramatic role of my career in *Pinky*," she admitted, "I was absolutely crushed when they cast me as a teenage ingénue in *Cheaper by the Dozen*. 'There are lots of things you don't understand,' Zanuck said. 'There will come a day, my dear, when no one will ask you to play a fifteen-year old.' Well, I accepted the role," she continued, "and the whole thing turned out to be a joyful association."

One factor in making the production a "joyful association" was getting to work with Myrna Loy, who played her mother in the film. Jeanne held the veteran actress "in such awe" that she was intimidated at the idea of working with her. According to Crain, "It wasn't easy working on an intimate family picture with someone you worship." Loy, however, put the younger star at ease and they got along very well, despite Jeanne having her name above Myrna's in the film's credits. Their co-star, Clifton Webb, was not as easy to get along with, causing Jeanne to describe him as "very temperamental, bombastic, and dictatorial." She recalled, "Myrna was the perfect foil for Clifton, letting him fly all over the place, while she remained serene and submissive and really in charge of the whole thing." While she felt her career was regressing with her teenage role as Ann Gilbreth, Zanuck still realized her box-office potential after the success of *Pinky*, and intended to take full advantage of it, while still looking after his young star's best interest.

A short story had come to the attention of Joseph Mankiewicz in April 1949, which he suggested to Zanuck as a potential film. Fox purchased the story, called *The Wisdom of Eve*, and it was given to Mankiewicz to write and direct, as he had done with *A Letter to Three Wives*. By early autumn, Mankiewicz had developed a screen treatment, which he titled *Best Performance* and passed on to Zanuck for approval. After reading the screenplay, which was retitled *All About Eve*, Zanuck wanted to produce it himself and noted the following casting possibilities: For the chief parts of

Jeanne and Paul having fun in the snow, 1949
(Courtesy of the Jeanne Crain Brinkman Family Trust)

Margo Channing and Addison DeWitt, Marlene Dietrich and Jose Ferrer and for the plum role of Eve Harrington, Jeanne Crain. Mankiewicz strongly objected to two of the three. He later recalled, "I was, and am, a great admirer of Marlene. But from what I knew of her work and equipment as an actress, I simply could not visualize — or 'hear' — her as a possible Margo." Instead, the director wanted movie veteran Claudette Colbert for the role, and with Zanuck in accord, she was signed for it in February 1950.

As for the producer's choice of Jeanne to play Eve, Mankiewicz was "deeply disappointed," and stood up to Zanuck, saying, "Darryl, you screwed up with *A Letter to Three Wives*." He continued, "There was no way she could get into the heart... if that's the right word... of Eve." His argument against the casting, was that Jeanne was "a sincere, honest, young actress." He explained, "Those aspects of Eve are obvious in her - but also, they are her. And there lies the rub. Crain, to my mind, is incapable of understanding - much less portraying - the burning, ruthless, driving and at times evil force that is the core of Eve."

By February, Hollywood columnist Sheila Graham had proclaimed that Jeanne was set for the part of the "eager-beaver young actress," but Mankiewicz warned the studio boss that he was putting his foot down on this issue and going to "scream and holler" until he got his way. Zanuck finally agreed to his plea that he could not elicit from Crain the degree of "bitch virtuosity" needed to play Eve, and finally approved Mankiewicz' suggestion of Anne Baxter, also under contract to the studio at the time. During these discussions, Jeanne discovered that she was again pregnant and according to Anne Baxter's account of casting the role, it was Crain's pending maternity leave that won her the coveted role of Eve Harrington. Baxter said Mankiewicz "owed" her one when her role as the original fourth wife was cut from *A Letter to Three Wives*.

Eve wasn't the only role that Crain lost due to pregnancy during 1950. In early spring, preparations were being made for *I'd Climb the Highest Mountain*, a drama about a young minister and his city-girl bride who are sent to work with mountain folk in the Ozarks. Jeanne was cast as the young wife, reunited with William Lundigan, her male co-star in *Pinky*, and scheduled to go to the mountains of northern Georgia for location shooting when she announced her condition. She was replaced by Susan Hayward. Another A-list production that had her name momentarily attached was *Carrie*. The film's director William Wyler was interested in Jeanne for the title role of Theodore Dreiser's story *Sister Carrie*. With the Fox actress unavailable, the part went to Jennifer Jones, who ironically was also pregnant, though she didn't reveal her condition until filming had begun. Jones miscarried shortly after completing the movie, and it was not released until 1952.

Cheaper by the Dozen was released in April and was Fox's biggest hit of 1950. It was the second year in a row that Jeanne had starred in the studio's top grossing film. Crain's only other film appearance that year was *I'll Get By*, a musical starring June Haver in which Jeanne made a cameo appearance as herself. She spent the summer away from the studio preparing for the birth of her third child, and on August 2, Timothy Peter joined his two brothers in the Brinkman family. Jeanne's close friend, actress Ann Blyth, was named as the child's godmother. Preparing for her return to the studio and her next picture, Crain worked out with Terry Hunt, the Beverly Hills health club owner and trainer to the stars, whose program of diet, massage and exercise could "whittle a pound a day off any client's weight."

Although confiding to a Hollywood columnist that she thought it was "about time for a bad girl role," her next movie had the actress playing yet another school girl, though she had just passed her twenty-fifth birthday. It was a step up, age wise, from *Cheaper by the Dozen*, as the character was a college freshman. Zanuck had vowed as the new decade began "to make as many pictures dealing with the problems of modern day life as we can find." Filming for *Take Care of My Little Girl* began in October, and with it, Zanuck saw another opportunity to address a social issue: the negative side of sororities and fraternities. Not nearly as serious or widespread a problem as those presented in *Gentleman's Agreement* or *Pinky*, it did, however, make for an interesting, if not overly dramatic endeavor.

Jeanne plays Liz Erickson, a beautiful, outgoing and socially prominent girl who sets off for college with her best friend, Janet. For all her attributes, Liz is also sheltered and naïve about the prejudices of social class. Liz and Janet hit Midwestern University ready to pledge the Tri-U (Upsilon, Upsilon, Upsilon) sorority, the "best" house on campus and the one in which Liz's mother was a member, some twenty years before. The "perfect" candidate, Liz easily becomes a pledge, but Janet does not come across as well and isn't accepted, the first crack in the veneer of Liz's idyllic view of the privileged sisterhood.

It doesn't take long for the boys to notice the freshman cutie and Liz dates two young men who are on opposite ends of the spectrum in personality and personal philosophy. Joe Blake (Dale Robertson) is a college senior and former soldier who is no fan of the Greek cliques and their superficial snobbery. Chad Carnes (Jeffrey Hunter) is her other beau, a drunken, womanizing frat boy who persuades Crain's Liz to help him cheat on an exam. Her unsavory involvement in Chad's cheating charade impresses one of her sorority sisters, the very chic and very haughty Dallas Prewitt (Jean Peters)

Jeanne with Dale Robertson in
Take Care of My Little Girl (1951)

and puts her in contention for the coveted title of Frosh Queen. By the film's last reel, Liz realizes what a shallow and callous bunch she has joined and chooses instead the company of the handsome and down-to-earth Joe.

Susan Hayward, who had replaced Jeanne in *I'd Climb the Highest Mountain*, was originally set to play Liz, but Crain's current popularity, thanks to her success in *Pinky* and *Cheaper by the Dozen,* landed her the lead. When it was released in July, *Take Care of My Little Girl* did well at the box-office, grossing an estimated $16,000 on its first day at the Roxy Theater in New York, the best opening day to that date in 1951, confirmation of Jeanne's continued audience appeal. The *New York Times'* Bosley Crowther noted both the winsome star's performance and her physical beauty, claiming she "plays the heroine with considerable expressiveness and charm, [and] is still pretty much of a model of feminine perfection all around."

Jeanne was getting impatient for meatier roles than the studio was assigning her. In her estimation, she "was the only actress in Hollywood with a husband and babies who wasn't allowed to mature on the screen." She wanted out of the "gingham and pigtail" roles for which she was most associated. After *Pinky,* she had had a taste of a truly dramatic character and she wanted more. She petitioned for a prime part in an upcoming production headed by Zanuck, which was being written and directed by Joe Mankiewicz. After the huge success of *All About Eve,* Mankiewicz could have his pick of film projects and he chose a German play called *Dr. Praetorius,* about a brilliant and unconventional gynecologist who stops the suicide of a young, unwed mother. It was the role of the pregnant girl that interested Crain, but when the leads were cast, it was her Fox rival, Anne Baxter, who was cast, with Cary Grant as Dr. Praetorius. However, when Baxter announced that she was expecting a baby, Zanuck gave Jeanne the part. (Although their screen personas were quite different, Crain and Baxter seemed to be interchangeable throughout their early careers, regularly being cast in parts when one or the other was unavailable.) Mankiewicz was less than pleased. Baxter had given an Oscar-nominated performance in *All About Eve* and was the director's personal choice for both that role and the one in his current production. He hadn't been happy with Jeanne in *A Letter to Three Wives* and he didn't relish working with her again. Unlike his pleadings with Zanuck over Crain's casting in *Eve*, this time his objections were overruled. He conceded, explaining:

> "It was probably my fault, but I could only rarely escape the feeling that Jeanne was, somehow, a visitor to the set. She worked hard. Too hard at times, I think, in response to my demands, as if trying to compensate by sheer exertion for what I believe must have been an absence of emotional involvement with acting. I wouldn't think she took the role home with her at night; she would assume it, rather, every morning with her wardrobe change for the day. I remember Jeanne Crain as a very pleasant, very shy, and very devout young woman, mother, and wife whose husband was doing very well in some business. She was one of the few whose presence among the theatre-folk I have never fully understood."

Years later, while reflecting on his association with the actress, and the two films on which they worked together, the director was less diplomatic. Regarding the coincidence of Crain's characters both being named Deborah in his movies he exclaimed: "I don't like the name Deborah and I don't like Jeanne Crain." If he could not change her method of acting, Mankiewicz did change her outer presence for the camera, instructing that her trademark long tresses be cut short and changing out the peasant blouses and skirts, of which she was so fond in her own wardrobe, for a tailored, chic look. She had always worn her hair long out of deference to Paul, who preferred it that way, but after the studio tested her in six wigs of different length, the final result was a medium bob. Excited about her new, more adult role, Jeanne sent a large bottle of champagne to Mankiewicz with a card attached that read: "If I fail you, you may pickle me in this!"

The Production Code Administration did not ignore the fact that the film (which was renamed *People Will Talk*) dealt with the sensitive subjects of unwed motherhood and suicide. Initially deemed unacceptable by PCA head Joseph Breen, due to its treatment of taboo subjects, revisions were made and a script was eventually approved. Breen was very clear, however, that no reference to abortion be made in the completed movie. The characters of Praetorius and Deborah do discuss the unborn child, though the word "abortion" is never used. Jeanne received decent reviews for her role as Deborah, including *Variety's* take, which observed both she and Grant "turn in the kind of performances expected of them." The box-office receipts were disappointing, however, and the general consensus was that *People Will Talk* was a sophisticated gem by Mankiewicz but audiences overall weren't that impressed.

1951 was a busy year for the young star with three pictures in release and one in production by year's end. A proposed film tentatively titled *The Jane Froman Story* was scheduled with Jeanne in the lead. It was the story of the famed singer who survived a 1943 airplane crash and was touted as Fox's biggest musical since *Alexander's Ragtime Band*. By the time it made it to the screen a year later, the project was called *With a Song in My Heart* and Susan

Hayward had been assigned the role, after Miss Froman voiced a preference for her. Besides *Take Care of My Little Girl* and *People Will Talk*, Jeanne starred in *The Model and the Marriage Broker*. Although she played the Model, it was the Marriage Broker, played by Thelma Ritter, who garnered the spotlight in the entertaining comedy-drama. Directed by George Cukor, who had worked with Jeanne in *Winged Victory*, it was a minor film compared to those usually overseen by Cukor, but one he made to fulfill a contractual obligation at Fox. Along with an ultra-chic wardrobe, Jeanne was allowed the services of top New York model Zori Jennings to coach her in "the fine art of live fashion display." Once the film was completed, Cukor sent a letter to Zanuck summarizing his pleasant experience on the *Marriage Broker* set, especially with Jeanne.

Despite her "grown up" roles in films directed by giants of the field like Mankiewicz and Cukor, in the summer of 1951, it was announced that Crain would be filming the sequel to *Cheaper by the Dozen*, called *Belles on Their Toes*. She reprised her role as eldest Gilbreth daughter, Ann, although this time around her character was older and much of the story revolved around her romance with Jeffrey Hunter, with whom she worked in *Take Care of My Little Girl*. As his character, the patriarch of the Gilbreth clan, had died in the first film, Clifton Webb didn't appear in its sequel, making for a more relaxed working environment during filming. Regarding the time on the set, Jeanne later recalled:

> "If you got along well the first time a sequel's like a family reunion. Clifton Webb, being the way he was, kind of set the tenor on *Cheaper by the Dozen*, but Myrna became the dominant one in the sequel. So

we were all much closer and the set was more festive… Since Myrna's character really came into flower, and mine grew up, we had more of a mother-daughter relationship in the script and on the set, too."

During filming Jeanne became pregnant and when *Belles on Their Toes* wrapped up in early November, she informed the studio that she was expecting her baby the following June. The AP wire wasted no time printing the announcement and also reported that with three growing boys, the Brinkmans hoped the child would be a girl. Their wish came true and on March 5, 1952, Jeanne gave birth to a daughter. Weighing in at seven pounds and nine ounces, the baby was named Jeanine Cherie. She wanted another baby, so Jeanine was a blessing, but her career was still lacking. She wanted the satisfaction she had experienced after making *Pinky* and the frustration of her current standing at Fox was undeniable. Changes had to be made.

{ 10 }
Goodbye, Fox

If Jeanne's career was not ideal in early 1952, Paul's was prosperous and thriving. He had shifted his business focus from radio manufacturing to more advanced electronic components, and opened a tool-and-die company in the late '40s. ABC Die and Engineering developed precision units, radar transmissions and valves. With the acquisition of government defense contracts to produce aircraft parts, he bought a parcel of property on North La Brea Avenue from the University of California, to erect a 12,000-square foot manufacturing plant. Although she knew little of the actual mechanics of the business (describing her husband's firm as one which "makes pistons and things that make motors go"), Jeanne served as its secretary/treasurer due to the legal benefits of having a family-run concern. Paul had business cards printed up with her name and title on them, but she did little in the decision-making process of the organization, which had its name changed to The Brinkman Manufacturing Company, Inc.

Back at Fox, Jeanne was scheduled to appear in an all-star vehicle entitled *O. Henry's Full House*. The film was divided into episodes, each based on a short story by the famed writer. Crain starred, with Farley Granger, in the most famous of the stories, "The Gift of the Magi," a Christmas tale of a poor young couple whose self-sacrifice ensures the other's happy Yuletide. With the other segments featuring Anne Baxter, Charles Laughton and Marilyn Monroe among the cast, there was strong marquee power, but the movie was weak, and one review found the performance of Crain and Granger lacking, saying they "sadly miss the freshness and humour of the young couple."

The big project currently taking shape at the studio was a large scale Biblical epic called *The Robe*. Zanuck had purchased the rights to it from RKO for a reported $100,000. Set in Rome during the time of the crucifixion of Jesus, the film featured a beautiful love interest named Diana, which was the part that interested Jeanne. She lobbied for the role, as she had done for others in the past, but when casting was complete, brunette star Jean Simmons was chosen. Sorely disappointed, Crain dyed her hair red in an attempt to "get away from juvenile roles." Producer Leonard Goldstein thought it was just the right look for his new Technicolor western called *Fight Town*. It wasn't *The Robe*, and although Jeanne wasn't excited about "the idea of playing a sagebrush heroine," she conceded that the part was more grown up than most of her recent roles. "I even get to slap Dale Robertson's [her leading man] face," she proclaimed, "my first screen slap." *Fight Town*, like so many films in the early stages of production, had its title changed before being released. It became *City of Bad Men*, a fictionalized account of the 1897 championship heavyweight fight between James J. Corbett and Bob Fitzsimmons.

The picture was filmed in December 1952 and by the end of January, Jeanne was on the set of her next movie, *Cabin B-13*. The title would be changed to *Dangerous Crossing*, a low-budget suspenser, which was developed to utilize the expensive sets built for the studio's big-budget drama, *Titanic*. The film found Crain as a wealthy new bride being given the "gaslight" treatment on board a luxury liner. Based on a radio play by John Dickson Carr, it was published in *Ellery Queen's Mystery Magazine* in May 1944, before finally making it to the screen almost a decade later. When the picture was released, reception was lukewarm at best, and Jeanne's performance followed suit, with a *New York Times* reviewer proclaiming that the actress was "beautiful but not entirely convincing in the role."

Jeanne and her growing family: Michael, Paul Jr., Timothy, Paul and Jeanine
(Courtesy of the Jeanne Crain Brinkman Family Trust)

She went almost immediately into her next movie, a remake of the studio's mystery-thriller, *I Wake Up Screaming*. The original film was produced in 1942 and starred Betty Grable in one of her few non-musical pictures. The new version was called *Vicki* and co-starred fellow Fox beauty, Jean Peters, with whom Crain had worked on *Take Care of My Little Girl*. Peters was a year younger than Jeanne, and well-liked among her Fox co-workers. She and Crain became close friends, and it was Jeanne to whom she confided her problems with future husband, billionaire Howard Hughes (In turn, Hughes would make numerous 3 a.m. calls to Jeanne during his troubled time with Jean Peters. These nocturnal conversations took place while Crain and her family were on vacation, and Paul was still in Los Angeles).

Like its predecessor, *Vicki* was a dark suspense story of a waitress who makes good as a fashion model, only to be murdered. Peters played the title role, while Jeanne played her protective, older sister. Both actresses were extremely attractive, but, as one biographer noted, the comparison between the characters wasn't "beautiful versus pretty, but delicate versus coarse; Crain is the lovelier of the two, but Peters has a tough sex appeal." *Vicki* was tagged as "contrived and far-fetched," and Jeanne's career benefitted nothing from her part in it. For this she had missed out on starring in *The Robe*? A film which was coming along as one of the biggest productions Fox had developed so far that decade.

Her misfortune of losing quality roles wasn't always the fault of the studio or her state of motherhood. In March, it was announced that she, along with Barbara Stanwyck and Gene Tierney, would star in *Three Coins in the Fountain*, a glamorous love story which was being shot in Rome that summer. When Jeanne told Paul about being assigned a role in the upcoming production, he refused to let her go on location in Europe, and the part was cast with Jean Peters.

She was disappointed, but in an attempt to compensate, Paul built Jeanne a small studio on a hill above their main house. Painting was still an endeavor she enjoyed, as well as compiling elaborate scrapbooks. To her private retreat she would go for quiet time, away from the stresses of family and work, to paint, unwind and generally rejuvenate. She even claimed to take nude moon baths there on warm nights. "I have solved many of my most difficult problems lying alone up on my hill beneath the moon and the stars," she said.

Her career seemed to be going nowhere. She had longed desperately to get away from the goody-two-shoe ingénue roles, only to be placed in second rate programmers. *City of Bad Men, Dangerous Crossing* and *Vicki* were all released in the autumn of 1953, but by that time Jeanne would already have parted ways with the studio for which she had worked an entire decade, and with which her name had been solidly associated. She had never made a motion picture at any studio other than Twentieth Century-Fox. They had hired her when she was seventeen years-old, less than a year out of high school, given her a screen persona and made her a star, but the time had come.

"I loved being at the studio," she said, "but there comes a time when an actress stays too long in the same place. People get used to having you around, and they can't think of you in a different light." She hadn't forgotten how Fox had squelched her hopes to star in *Carrie* and *Quo Vadis* (in the role eventually played by Deborah Kerr), both projects requiring a loan-out to other studios. Nor had she forgotten being rejected for *The Robe*. She acknowledged that her home lot had been "wonderful" to her, but also admitted to not being happy her last years there. "I wasn't permitted to go to other studios on loan-outs," she said. "Other girls were signed for roles I wanted at my own studio. I asked for singing and dancing roles, but the answer always was 'No.' Now, after 10 years, maybe I'll get my big chance."

She began getting offers for work within hours of the news breaking that she had left her former, long term stomping grounds. Her departure from the studio wasn't without financial consequences, however. Had her final option been picked up for another year, Crain's salary would have jumped to $5,000 per week, and she ultimately paid Fox $50,000 to release her from her contract. The studio's roster of stars was changing and Jeanne wasn't alone in going through its doors. Her co-star and friend, Linda Darnell was released in 1952, and Tyrone Power, along with the company's top box-office draw of the previous decade, Betty Grable, would leave within two years. The Brinkmans were comfortable enough financially for Jeanne to take the leap, with Paul reportedly netting $90,000 the same year as his wife's departure from her home studio.

Immediately after ending her contract with Fox, Jeanne made an appointment with one of the most successful press agents in Hollywood, Russell Birdwell. It was Birdwell who had spearheaded the campaign that included the search for Scarlett O'Hara in the late '30s, when casting for *Gone with the Wind* was at the top of the nation's pop culture radar. She explained that she was tired of the America's Sweetheart image that hung around her neck and wanted to create a new, sexy persona which she hoped would lead to more exciting roles. She then made a drastic change. She cut her hair even shorter than she had done for *People Will Talk*. After consulting with one of the models she worked with on *The Model and the Marriage Broker* about her own chic, short coiffure, Crain made an appointment at Bentley's Salon in Beverly Hills, where she received what would be called the Bob Cat Bob, a disheveled 'do that "reeked of abandon but was very smart." She then "tossed away her Peter Pan collars for plunging necklines," a look, in combination with her sleek haircut, that she hoped to impress upon producers as her new, sultry image. Her transformation didn't get lost on Louella Parsons, who reported that "Jeanne Crain's hair gets redder and shorter by the minute." There were also some longtime fans who didn't care for the "new look," including an Ohio matron who opined, "Bring back our old, lovely Jeanne minus *that* hair-cut and *those* short skirts."

Socially, Jeanne and Paul became even more active. Although they had never been hermits in Hollywood, they lived a quieter night life together in the early years of their marriage. Crain explained that when she began making movies, she was still a teenager, living with Loretta, who monitored her social life and hours to be home. Then, when she and Paul married, their focus was on building their dream house and eventually having babies. All this combined with her very active work schedule at Fox. Now, trying to break free from her "America's sweetheart" image, she wore her new look around the Tinsel Town hotspots regularly. She became such a staple that a Hollywood Reporter columnist observed she was "the one gal I see at EVERY Hollywood party," and months later noted that she attended "more parties than any other gal in town."

Jeanne admitted that, after working so steadily at Fox, she was enjoying herself, saying: "I'm past 25, I'm married and the mother of four, and, for the first time in my life, you really see me everywhere these days. I go out on the slightest pretext – and I love it." It wasn't long before she gained the reputation of Hollywood's Number One Party Girl. "I get invited to at least 200 parties a year," Jeanne proclaimed. "I can't go to all of them, of course, so I try to make the ones that sound like the most fun. We like the small parties at friends' home [sic] the best," she added. "But there are more kinds of parties in Hollywood than there are makes of cars. The ones that make the most news are the spectaculars like the tremendous affairs Sonja Henie throws."

Armed with confidence, eagerness and a new image, her first screen role, after leaving Fox, was announced as a sequel to the studio's *Gentlemen Prefer Blondes*, a musical-comedy starring Jane Russell and up-and-coming bombshell Marilyn Monroe. *Blondes* hadn't even been released yet when Jeanne's involvement with its follow-up film was announced. The picture was called *Gentlemen Marry Brunettes* and, like its predecessor, was based on a story by former flapper and prolific screenwriter Anita Loos. The new picture wasn't, however, to be a Twentieth Century-Fox production, instead being made independently by a British company called Film Locations, Ltd. The film was to be shot in London and was planned to be the first British movie to be made in the new 3-D process, as well as wide screen and Technicolor. It was a financial boon for Crain, who would receive $65,000 in cash, $25,000 in escrow and $5,000 for European expenses. Like *Blondes*, the movie centered around two beautiful women, a sister-act, traveling Europe. Debbie Reynolds was slated to co-star with Jeanne, and both were excited about their first trip across the pond. In turn, both were disappointed when it was announced that the production date had been postponed.

With *Gentlemen Marry Brunettes* on the back burner, Crain's post-Fox debut was a complete change of pace, though it still allowed her to travel overseas. *Duel in the Jungle* was an action-adventure picture that had Jeanne paired again with her *State Fair* leading man, Dana Andrews. Filming was to take place in England and Africa, the latter a dream destination for both Brinkmans. Unlike her lost role in *Three Coins in the Fountain*, this time Paul not only allowed Jeanne to take the part on location overseas, but planned to accompany her and in August, the couple sailed for Europe on the *S.S. Liberte*. Filming in Africa was anything but glamorous. A makeup call was scheduled every morning at 5 am, followed by a day of tramping through jungles and swamps. Then a special sunset shot was set up every evening at 6:30. An hour later, an exhausted cast and crew would make its way back to their hotel where they would dine, take a hot bath and study the next day's script before falling to sleep at 9:30.

Tragedy struck while filming near Livingstone Falls in North Rhodesia, when first assistant director, Tony Kelly, was killed in an accident on the Zambesi River. Kelly, along with two other technicians, an African aide and camera equipment, was in an outboard-motored dinghy, scouting locations down river when the boat foundered in the swift-flowing rapids and sank almost immediately. Two of the men swam ashore, while a third made it after battling a whirlpool, but Kelly went down and his body was never recovered. It was suggested that he was trying to save some of the equipment. Jeanne and the others on the rivers bank witnessed the event. Later, she admitted how close she herself had come to being affected personally by the tragic accident. Paul had asked to go with the men in the boat but was refused permission by the film's director, George Marshall, as too dangerous. Jeanne later recalled that he was "mad as blazes" then realized how lucky he had been.

Jeanne meeting Queen Elizabeth II in 1953
(Courtesy of the Jeanne Crain Brinkman Family Trust)

In October, after location filming in Africa was completed, Jeanne and Paul made a three-day stopover in Italy, and Jeanne fell in love with the country. Always enamored with the Renaissance masters, to be in the country that gave birth to and nurtured their talent was a magical experience for the actress, and one she would revisit every chance she was able. The couple barely slept during their short respite, for fear of missing a single experience. They then went on to England, where interior shooting was done at London's Elstree Studios. Later the same month, Crain, along with fellow actors Gary Cooper, Richard Basehart and Joanne Dru, was presented to the newly coronated Queen Elizabeth II, during a royal screening of *Rob Roy*. The Hollywood delegation was rendered relatively speechless during the elegant, formal event. "Gosh, darn it," Cooper told reporters afterward, "I was reduced to my usual 'yep' and 'nope' just when I wanted to be eloquent." Jeanne reflected a similar experience. "I was too excited to answer," she said, "But I was proud I remembered to say 'your majesty.'"

In February 1954, with filming complete on *Duel in the Jungle* and production on *Gentlemen Marry Brunettes* still not ready to begin, Jeanne agreed to a five-year contract with Universal-International to make one picture a year. Her first movie, *Tacey Cromwell*, would be a big-budget western to be produced by Ross Hunter, and star Crain in the title role. Universal had carried the reputation as a low-budget, low-quality, low-man-on-the-Hollywood-totem pole company for years, focusing on its iconic horror and science fiction product. But in the late '40s and 1950s, after a merger with independent International Pictures, the company began putting more focus on quality over quantity and revamped its image, showcasing tear-jerking women's pictures by director Douglas Sirk, inexpensive but highly profitable comedy series like *Ma and Pa Kettle* and *Francis the Talking Mule*, and colorful, epic westerns.

In late April, Jeanne signed her contract with Universal-International, with the final terms specifying the star's appearance in three pictures, while being paid $865.38 a week for 260 weeks. She would be free to continue freelancing between other studios the rest of the time. This would allow her to be selective of her roles, as well as spend more time with Paul and the children. When *Tacey Cromwell* finally began filming, its title was changed to *One Desire* and Jeanne's old, role-swapping pal, Anne Baxter, got the part.

In May 1954, while waiting for her first picture at her new studio, Jeanne appeared on television for the first time. She was the mystery guest on the popular CBS game show, *What's My Line?* Looking very chic and using a Tallulah Bankhead-esque voice to try and fool the blind-folded celebrity panel, she kept them guessing until show regular, Bennett Cerf, asked if she had "several little babies of your own" in private life, which immediately gave away her identity. She had fun and would appear on the show for a second time five years later, even more comfortable and confident in front of television cameras (and again outed by Cerf).

The same month as her first *What's My Line?* appearance, Jeanne revisited her past, collaborating again with her former mentor, photographer William Mortensen. Her days as a model for the non-traditional artist weren't discussed much during her early years in the film industry. A decade later, however, the two came together to create a set of one-hundred new photos, which would mirror the same number of identical poses from 1942. Both the originals and the new shots were enlarged and exhibited in a Hollywood gallery in May. When Mortensen passed away in 1965, Jeanne, along with Vincent Price, would narrate a documentary on his career called *Monsters and Madonnas*.

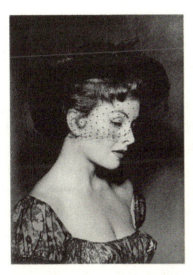

Jeanne from the 1953 William Mortensen photography session
(Courtesy of the Jeanne Crain Brinkman Family Trust)

With *Tacey Cromwell* going to Anne Baxter, Crain's first picture for Universal was another big-budget western called *Man Without a Star*, co-starring Kirk Douglas, with whom she had worked in *A Letter to Three Wives* in 1948. As Reed Bowman, a beautiful but cold-hearted ranch owner in the Old West, Jeanne finally got to play the kind of "bad girl" she had long waited for. Filming began in June and continued throughout the summer. Directed by veteran King Vidor and filmed in Technicolor, the studio had high hopes for its success and Jeanne needed a hit, as *Duel in the Jungle* opened in early August to poor reviews. The *New York Times* called it "as feeble and contrived a safari drama as has come along in some time." Another industry scribe observed the "good production values and fine Technicolor photography are not enough to lift this action melodrama above the level of routine entertainment."

After waiting more than a year for production to begin on *Gentlemen Marry Brunettes*, cameras finally rolled on the picture in September. Since Jeanne had signed on for the film, the production had been taken over by Russ-Field Corp., a newly formed company led by actress Jane Russell (Russ) and her husband, former football star Robert Waterfield (Field). It was the debut production for the fledgling operation, which made a deal with distributor United Artists for six films, *Gentlemen Marry Brunettes* being the first. Russell would play the part initially scheduled for Debbie Reynolds and hopefully bring some of the success which had been showered on *Gentlemen Prefer Blondes*. Russell wasn't crazy about the property, feeling it was a big, expensive production which was being hung on her shoulders alone. Of her co-star, she later recalled: "Jeanne is a darling girl and had proven herself as an actress, but at the box office she wasn't a Marilyn Monroe." The picture was shot on location in Paris and Monte Carlo, then finishing with interior sequences at the Shepperton Studios outside London. As they had been during her years at Twentieth Century-Fox, her musical vocals were dubbed by someone else, this time singer Anita Ellis.

Crain fell in love with France and "everything French." Unlike the pre-dawn hours of preparation and long days of shooting in Africa, her European experience was quite different. "You start work at noon making a picture there," she explained, "and go until 8 pm without a break. It's the most divine way of working. In Hollywood, you don't mind getting up early – you get used to it – but who wants to start emoting at 9 am?" Paul made three trips to see Jeanne in Europe and in December, when the cast began shooting in England, he brought the children over from the United States, via commercial airline, so the family could experience a "real English Christmas" together. After the holiday, the entire family set sail on New Year's Day aboard the *Liberte* for a two-week voyage home.

If *Gentlemen Marry Brunettes* wanted to capture some of the magic created by *Gentlemen Prefer Blondes*, Jeanne's next film – her second for Universal-International – was ready to ride the coattails of the very popular MGM musical, *Seven Brides for Seven Brothers*, which had been released the previous summer. *The Second Greatest Sex* was based on an ancient tale, *Lysistrata*, by Aristophanes, and told the story of a small Kansas town in 1880, whose women withhold their "marital obligations" from their husbands because they feel ignored and taken for granted. It was a big splashy musical filmed in Cinemascope and Technicolor. George Nader was cast as Crain's handsome leading man. Ironically, it was Jeanne's mother, Loretta, who saw Nader as a young actor at the famed Pasadena Playhouse and introduced him to Jeanne. This led to a contract with Fox and a series of small parts – including *Take Care of My Little Girl*. By the time *The Second Greatest Sex* was released, Nader had not only secured a contract with Universal, but also won a Golden Globe as "Most Promising Newcomer." The picture also featured blonde sex kitten Mamie Van Doren and comedian Bert Lahr. It wasn't *Seven Brides for Seven Brothers*, but it was moderate fun.

Jeanne with Jane Russell in France during the filming of *Gentlemen Marry Brunettes*. Paul is standing in the background.
(Courtesy of the Jeanne Crain Brinkman Family Trust)

Both *Gentlemen Marry Brunettes* and *The Second Greatest Sex* premiered in October 1955. Although *Brunettes* was well-received, it couldn't make back the enormous amount that it had cost to make. Jeanne's performance, however, seemed to be a sultry surprise to many and the *New York Herald Tribune* praised her performance observing she been "hiding her light under a pinafore far too long." The film not only opened up her opportunity to enhance her new screen persona, it allowed her to expand her cultural horizons through her travels in Europe during the shooting time there (the trip also allowed Paul to buy a new Mercedes-Benz, which he had shipped back to the United States). Both of her recent films were big, musical spectacles, and her western with Kirk Douglas was profitable. Still, the pictures did not hold the same career magic as those during her years at Fox.

1956 began with a new movie, this time another western called *The Fastest Gun Alive*. It was made at MGM, a first for Jeanne. She had now made films for three of the major studios since leaving Twentieth Century-Fox. She and Glenn Ford co-starred in the above-average character study, with Ford playing a peaceful, brooding storekeeper in a western town, whose prowess with a firearm is exceptional. The problem is that having such skill draws potential gun-slinging challengers from far and wide, making a normal life impossible for the merchant and his patient wife, played by Crain.

It was a positive experience for Jeanne, who called Glenn Ford "one of the finest actors with whom I've ever played," and claimed the film's director, Russell Rouse, was "so good looking all the hairdressers and secretaries used to make excuses to come on our set." Production on *The Fastest Gun Alive* began in January and while Jeanne was gearing up for her role, Paul was supervising the move into their new home.

As the family was growing, the Brinkmans purchased a house on North Roxbury Drive in Beverly Hills. Previously owned by Warner Brothers director, Michael Curtiz, the four-bedroom property totaled over 7,900 square feet and was on the same street as Rosemary Clooney and Jose Ferrer, the Jack Bennys and Lucille Ball and Desi Arnaz. Paul had just sold his airplane parts company on La Brea Avenue for a tidy profit and was contemplating a potential real estate business, a venture he had taken on successfully before he married Jeanne.

At the end of February, when filming was completed on *The Fastest Gun Alive,* the couple had planned a vacation to Sun Valley, Idaho, but switched their destination for Honolulu instead. "This won't be like most of our other trips," Paul insisted. "Usually, Jeanne was on studio business, and they lived our lives for us. This time, we'll be on our own." The Hawaii trip was planned so that an extensive redecorating job could be completed on the new house in Beverly Hills while they were gone. They had enjoyed an extended vacation the previous summer, after Jeanne finished up on the three movies she made during 1955. She and Paul had spent several weeks in South America, something they had "always wanted to do." But before that jaunt, Jeanne spent a month in Laguna Beach, reading, swimming, painting and relaxing in the sun. Little did she know that during this peaceful time of rest and sunbathing, events were unfolding that would bring drastic changes to her life as she knew it.

{ 11 }
Divorce Court

The cover featured a photo of Frank Sinatra with the caption, "WHY SINATRA IS THE TARZAN OF THE BOUDOIR," as well as a candid snapshot of Jane Russell. On page 10, there was a black and white photo of Jeanne, looking very chic, in a form-fitting, sleeveless dress, but with a harsh look on her face. The headline read: **What did the Starlet have that the Star *didn't* have? ASK JEANNE CRAIN'S HUBBY!** It was the latest issue of *Confidential* magazine, considered the granddaddy of the scandal sheets, which, by 1955, had reached five million copies per issue with a larger circulation than *Reader's Digest, Ladies' Home Journal, Look, The Saturday Evening Post* or *Collier's*. The article detailed Paul's alleged infidelity with an unnamed starlet, pinning him as "one of those duck-around daddies" and posing the question: "Why be a wolf when you already have one of the nation's cutest lambs at home?"

The article claimed that Brinkman met the girl at a cocktail party, which he and Jeanne had attended in July of the previous year, and began pursuing her shortly after. When questioned by the cutie what would happened if his wife caught them, Paul reportedly answered, "Don't worry, she's in Laguna and won't be home." The piece went on to say that after the Brinkmans' trip to South America, Paul called the starlet only to be told by her roommate that she wasn't home. With his original plan thwarted, he took the roommate out instead.

If Jeanne saw the story, it was a pre-release copy or she heard of it from insiders, because the issue was set for May, and on March 29, 1956, she stunned Hollywood when she filed for divorce from her husband after more than a decade of supposedly idyllic marriage. She retained high profile entertainment attorneys, Martin Gang and Milton A. Rudin, who filed the Superior Court action, which charged Paul with "extreme cruelty, and inflicting physical injury and violence without provocation." The suit also charged that Brinkman's conduct was "detrimental to her health, caused her mental anguish and interfered with her career." Crain asked for custody of the children, and as soon as the suit was filed, she left town and went into seclusion.

The Crain - Brinkman divorce made headlines across the country. How could this rarity, a happy and successful Hollywood marriage, one of the most solid in the film industry, fail? Jeanne claimed that the *Confidential* article had nothing to do with her decision, telling Louella Parsons that the situation with Paul had been "intolerable" for two years. Her strong Catholic faith and their children had been the basis of the front which she tried to hold up for so long. Brinkman blamed the split on family ill will from Loretta and Rita. "You remember the bitterness her mother felt at the time we eloped?" he said to Parsons. "For eleven years, I have had to battle family resentment."

The breakup came in the midst of the move into the new house on Roxbury Drive. The alterations to their new home would take six months to complete, and Paul and Jeanne had planned on renting a house in Laguna Beach for the summer.

The Confidential magazine piece that broke
in spring 1956
(Courtesy of Thomas Brown)

Just days before the divorce was filed, Parsons reported on the progress of the new décor in the Brinkman home, which offered four master suites. "We're tearing apart our new house in Beverly Hills," said Paul, and when asked what style, he replied, "South American modern. We're putting in plenty of glass." Jeanne still intended on moving in, but made different arrangements for the planned redecoration job. She also had her career to think of, despite all the tension of the divorce, especially during the raw early days of the period, when the hurt and shock were still fresh. A week after the filing, she had a sitting with world famous portrait photographer, Yousuf Karsh, for *Pix* magazine, which would feature other Hollywood beauties.

Paul saw the children on the weekends, but didn't see Jeanne, nor did he talk to her. Friends reported that Mrs. Brinkman "turned a deaf ear" to pleas of a second chance for Paul and their marriage, describing her as "quietly heartbroken, gallant and adamant." On May 8, Paul filed a demurrer to the pending divorce suit to force Jeanne to give details of her cruelty charges. He told the court that the complaint filed by his estranged wife was "uncertain, unintelligible and ambiguous." Brinkman got what he requested when Jeanne dropped a bombshell which shocked the film colony. On May 16, Crain's attorney filed an amended complaint in Los Angeles Superior Court, charging her husband with beating her into unconsciousness, abuse and having affairs with other women. The eleven-page bill of particulars included other bitter allegations.

One complaint included Loretta and illustrated that the old emotional wounds created when Jeanne first married were not healed. Jeanne claimed: Paul "held my mother up to ridicule at social functions and in front of our friends and called her a parasite," and on Christmas day, he dragged his wife out of a phone booth, where she was trying to call her mother. Regarding the couple's financial situation, Jeanne stated that he forced her to support the entire family, giving her a "feeling of insecurity, since a star's position is always precarious." She said she had stated a desire to spend more time with their children and less at the studio. When she remarked on more than one occasion that her star billing "wouldn't last forever," she alleged that Brinkman insisted that she resume work as soon as possible after the birth of each child. She said she once asked him to sign a separate property agreement under which her earnings would be her separate property, but he refused because "he wouldn't waive his right to alimony." Regarding the accusation of Brinkman's infidelities with other women, Jeanne said that when charged with the action in a scandal magazine [*Confidential*], he "never denied the truth of the charges and his sole reaction has been one of self-pity."

The accusations of physical and sexual abuse included an incident on March 17, when the plaintiff went to four-year-old Jeanine's bedroom and locked the door, followed by Brinkman, who pounded on the door and demanded that it be opened. When it wasn't, he burst through and entered the bedroom. Crain claimed she tried to escape but was seized by her husband who beat her, grabbing her head while she was on her knees and forcing it back until it touched the floor. Her vertebrae seemed to crack and she lost consciousness.

On another occasion, he allegedly struck her when she censured him for hitting one of their children in the face. The final straw came on March 28, when, according to Crain, her husband beat her unconscious, ripping off her clothes and threatening to disfigure her so that "she would never work again and no man would ever look at her again." She was later hospitalized. The following day the divorce suit was filed. The amended suit was met with newspaper stories outlining Brinkman's "cave-man love tactics," and surprise at what had mistakenly seemed like a decade-long dream marriage.

Paul responded that he was "deeply shocked" at the "wild, irresponsible and untrue" accusations. He announced that he "had no choice" but to sue Jeanne for divorce on his own charges and indicated the battle "may turn into Hollywood's liveliest divorce fight in years." He admitted he and Jeanne had "certain disputes concerning her mother," but went on to say that his mother-in-law was "hostile" to him and was "trying to break up the marriage."

On Friday, May 18, Jeanne appeared for a reconciliation hearing requested by her husband. She and Paul were separately interviewed by Superior Judge Lewis Drucker, who refused to comment on the case afterward. "There isn't any chance for reconciliation," Crain told the judge. "I feel the chance (for reconciliation) has gone by." Because of their children, California divorce laws provided that a case could be brought into reconciliation court if either party requested the action in an attempt to reconcile for the sake of the offspring. The following week, Paul threatened cross-complaint for divorce against Jeanne, though his attorney, Robert Powsner, stated it wouldn't be filed immediately. "Reconciliation hopes have dimmed," declared the lawyer, "but negotiations have been renewed to see if this matter can't be settled peaceably. If it can, Mr. Brinkman may not have to tell his full side of the story."

But, on June 1, Paul cracked the surface with his side. He asked the Superior Court to force his wife to abide by a prior stipulation, where Jeanne's attorney, Milton Rudin, verbally agreed that Brinkman could file an answer and cross-complaint in general terms with the right to amend them later. Jeanne had since refused to approve a written stipulation to the same effect, which would force her husband to make specific public charges, causing "widespread publicity." Paul said "I'll tell my side of the story," if his wife didn't shield their children from publicity.

A few days later, Crain's friend, Bobbie Kester, at whose home the Brinkmans met in 1943, told Jeanne that Paul was carrying a gun and "if worst comes to worst he will use it." She relayed to Jeanne what Brinkman told her in a recent conversation, saying that he was despondent because his estranged wife seemed indifferent to his welfare. "I told him that he was not the type to commit suicide," Mrs. Kester stated in an affidavit, "and he replied that he might and in that case, he would take Jeanne with him." Based on Kester's statement, Jeanne petitioned the court to take away any guns in Brinkman's possession. The petition also included a request that her husband be punished for contempt of court because of what she called, his violation of a restraining order issued by the court forbidding him to visit the couple's home, except to see their children. She said he had been there on numerous occasions during her absence and that early last month the housekeeper saw him attempting to tap her telephone line. According to Crain, he also had private detectives following her, and cashed checks on their community property. She gave their joint net worth as $226,900 and stated that she earned $2400 a month, after taxes and expenses the previous year.

A hearing was set to address all her requests for June 25. Paul's attorney, Robert Powsner, said both he and Brinkman regretted Crain's filing the new affidavit and added: "This is a deliberate attempt to torpedo our efforts at reaching a peaceful settlement and avoiding publicity... Apparently Mrs. Brinkman feels that the lurid publicity which will result from a wild and wooly battle will help her career. This is problematical, but it certainly will not help her children. Unfortunately, she has chosen her weapons. We will, if we must, answer her scurrilous charges and join in the battle." Powsner predicted "a real juicy hassle" when the divorce made it to trial. "She has forced us into this hassle and we will enter into it with full force," the attorney told reporters. He added that his client's cross-complaint would allege cruelty, which would be detailed and "other grounds," on which he declined to elaborate. Brinkman then hired Arthur Crowley. Once called "the toughest Irishman attorney west of Chicago," Crowley practically invented one of the central figures of the tabloid world: the celebrity divorce lawyer.

On June 14, Brinkman dropped a bombshell of his own, when Crowley filed a cross-complaint accusing Jeanne of an extramarital affair with Howard Hoch Rhoads, a married aircraft executive and a family friend. In the suit, Brinkman claimed his wife had been intimate with Rhoads "in the first three weeks of December 1955 in North Hollywood, on two occasions." He also charged that Rhoads and Crain had been together on several other occasions "in the City of Los Angeles." His suit stated that she was an "unfit and improper person," and he was therefore seeking custody of their four children.

Rhoads was the president of Hydro-Aire Co., a Burbank-based aircraft parts manufacturing plant. He had known the Brinkmans for years and vehemently denied the accusation. "Any charges of adultery are ridiculous," he said when informed of the suit. "Mrs. Brinkman has a spotless reputation," he continued. "She is s fine mother and an altogether nice person. Any such charges are pure fiction." He said his family and the Brinkmans had been neighbors in Beverly Hills for approximately eighteen months. "Our children play together," he said. "My wife knows Mrs. Brinkman. This apparently is a vindictive smear."

Jeanne also denied the charges, issuing a statement through her agent. "There is absolutely no truth to the charges. Paul cannot face the fact that the breakup of our marriage is due to his own actions, and so he has had to reach out for some straws in the wind." She also said, "He has already broken my heart, now he is trying to break my spirit." Brinkman's three-page cross-complaint also contained specific denials to the charges Jeanne made in her amended divorce suit. Regarding the issues addressing Loretta Crain's financial support from her daughter's film earnings, Paul asserted that his mother-in-law's financial demands were "unreasonable and unconscionable." He recalled an incident when Jeanne was making a picture in Europe, became ill and requested that her mother join her there for comfort. Brinkman claimed that Mrs. Crain remarked that she would rather have the money that the trip would cost to buy a luxury automobile. He further complained that Mrs. Crain screamed that she was putting an "Irish curse" on him and would do all in her power to break up the marriage.

The Hollywood columns didn't let the cross-complaint go by without a pass. One observer noted: "Paul Brinkman isn't getting as much sympathy here as he'd expected. That's not only because his estranged wife, Jeanne Crain, is no Marilyn Monroe – but also because Brinkman is definitely no Joe

DiMaggio." Crain's friends backed her and had no doubt that she had never "stepped out of line as Mrs. Paul Brinkman." Attorney Crowley planned to take Crain's deposition, forcing her to answer questions about her relationship with Rhoads.

After Paul's cross-complaint was filed, Jeanne fired her attorneys and hired one of the most powerful celebrity lawyers of the day, Greg Bautzer and his partner, Gerald Lipsky. Bautzer was a celebrity himself. A self-made man, who had represented the biggest names in Hollywood for years, as well as romancing its most beautiful and glamorous females, including Lana Turner, Joan Crawford and Ava Gardner. With Bautzer and Lipsky new to the case, they were not adequately prepared to argue the motions filed by Crain's previous attorneys. Bautzer told the press: "We have just recently been substituted in this case. We consider it a wiser strategy not to pursue these motions." On June 25, the motions dropped included Jeanne's request that her husband pay a specific amount for child support, that he be held in contempt of court for allegedly violating a restraining order, and that he surrender his guns to the court.

Three days later, Crain's 66-page deposition, which had been taken the previous week, was filed with the Superior Court. In it, Jeanne admitted that she kissed Rhoads "just once" – on his birthday, with both his wife, Hilda, and Brinkman present. She added that she was alone with the aircraft equipment manufacturer on two occasions in a North Hollywood apartment which she "understood" to be his secretary's. She declared, however, that nothing improper occurred. "It was a conversation about his drinking," she testified. "He and his wife were having trouble. They are both very good friends of ours," she added. "They weren't happy and felt that we were successfully and happily married." According to Crain, Rhoads was dressed in a business suit the entire time during the visit and they discussed her husband's attempt to help Rhoads through a "drinking spell" the previous August. She admitted to visiting Rhoads on another occasion a few weeks later, while keeping these visits from Brinkman for several weeks.

Jeanne refused to answer sixteen of the questions posed by Brinkman's attorney. These included questions about conversations with Rhoads' mother in which Crain said the woman was "acting like a cruel witch." She also did not answer whether or not she had said she had a "guilt complex" about the way she was treating her husband or about the way she "felt" about Rhoads. A court session was scheduled for July 11, at which Jeanne would be asked the unanswered questions from the earlier deposition. The session was canceled, however, when Brinkman surprisingly dropped the adultery charges and a peaceful settlement was reached in mid-July. The day the settlement was announced, a Hollywood column asked the question: "Weren't Paul Brinkman and Roma Page a twosome at the Luau? They were in the same party and walked out together."

Jeanne's publicity agent announced at the end of the month that a property settlement had been reached, as well as an agreement for a quiet divorce, which would not be contested by Brinkman. The couple signed a financial settlement which provided for equal division of community property and a $300 monthly child support payment by Paul, though Jeanne waived alimony. The divorce hearing was set for August 6. The same week it was announced that Jeanne would soon begin shooting her new picture under her

Universal-International deal. *The Tattered Dress* was to be shot in Cinemascope and costar popular leading man, Jeff Chandler. "I want to get involved in good, hard work," Crain told a reporter. "I want to be at a studio and not think of myself. I am going to try self-discipline. In time, I hope to learn about myself and my emotions."

On Monday, August 6, Jeanne "solemnly but tearlessly" divorced Paul. "My soul has been seared," she confessed after the ordeal, "but now I must build a new life and forge ahead." She admitted that she had been unhappy and troubled for some time. "When I worked at MGM last winter on *The Fastest Gun Alive*, I was in such a state of conflict personally I scarcely could work. Glenn Ford must have wondered why I was reading books on psychology and philosophy on the set. I was trying to hold myself together. I must be the kind of person who doesn't look the way she feels." If Jeanne was distraught due to the interlocutory decree, Paul was definitely moving forward. Within ten days of the hearing, he was reportedly dating starlet Gia Scala, who was described as looking "a little like Ingrid Bergman, a little like Grace Kelly, like Nancy Olson around the eyes, and like four or five of those sexy Italian actresses below the neck." By the end of the month, however, Scala "made a quick switcheroo" from Brinkman to Seth Baker, a New York City stockbroker who had recently divorced Jack Benny's daughter, Joan. The following week, Louella Parsons observed that Paul was seen "with this girl and that." One of the girls after Scala was raven-haired beauty, Laurette Luez. A "tall, dark, curvy Amazon," Luez had been groomed by Columbia a few years earlier for "sex-stardom," and made a succession of B-films, including 1950's *Prehistoric Women*. Paul saw her regularly throughout October, November and the early part of December, spotted at different night spots in Los Angeles.

Jeanne made it clear that she could not remain on friendly terms with her soon-to-be ex-husband. "I don't see how they can remain such casual 'good friends' about it," she said about ex-spouses. "It's a cliché about divorced couples saying 'We're still good friends.' It's impossible for me. It's like somebody taking a cleaver and going klops, kerflooey, down through your heart." She became emotionally exhausted after the break-up, losing weight and showing strain. In mid-October, she was admitted to St. John's Hospital, getting the "rest she was not able to get at home," stated her physician, Dr. John Egan. While at the hospital, part of her treatment was to regain some weight. She also still had to work. She was announced to co-star with Frank Sinatra in a feature for Paramount called *The Joker is Wild*, a dramatic bio-pic about nightclub comedian/singer Joe E. Lewis.

Then, in mid-December, Paul asked Jeanne to the annual New Year's Eve extravaganza hosted by millionaire David "Tex" Feldman. It was the same celebration which had been the couple's first official date in 1943. Friends hoped it could be the beginning of a permanent reconciliation, but on the day after Christmas, a pickup order was issued for Paul, who was accused of assaulting, with a deadly weapon, both Rhoads and his friend, Ted Ryan, a 38-year-old advertising executive. The scuffle took place in front of the Hollywood Hills apartment house where Rhoads lived and was hosting a Christmas party. Ryan told the police he and his girlfriend were leaving the party when he was attacked as he was getting in his car. Hearing his friend call for help, Rhoads rushed to the car, where Brinkman "turned on him and threw many punches" before leaving in his own car. Ryan, who was treated for a puncture wound on the cheek below his right eye, told officers that he believed Brinkman was carrying a knife.

Rhoads told reporters later that he intended on marrying Jeanne because "I'm in love with her and she's in love with me." With a cut forehead and skinned elbows and knees, he added: "This is a horrible way to make a wedding announcement, but that's the way it is." Brinkman said he went to Rhoads' apartment to ask him to stop interfering with his efforts toward reconciliation with his wife. Rhoads countered that the jealous husband "jumped me with some sort of a weapon" because "he knew about us." Rhoads also claimed he had given his wife a million dollars to divorce him in an effort to marry Jeanne. For her part, Crain said she had "no romantic interest in anyone." Brinkman surrendered the following day, pleading innocent to the charges. He was released on $500 bail and ordered to stand trial on February 15.

On New Year's Eve, the Feldman party was a lavish $125,000 spectacle, held at Romanoff's in Hollywood. The nightspot's Crown Room was taken over for two days to be converted into a turn of the century Delmonico's. A seven-course dinner was served, with seven kinds of wine, and French singer Edith Piaf was the featured entertainment. Jeanne and Paul arrived together, arm in arm, and throughout the night, "the two were all smiles, obviously one of the most happy couples on the dance floor." Brinkman proclaimed to a reporter: "No one is happier than Jeanne and I and our four children over tonight." The children and the couple's Catholic beliefs were the reasons Jeanne gave for getting back together. "I hadn't intended to make any reconciliation announcement, but we have been quietly seeing each other for the past several weeks," the actress said. "We have been discussing our problems and trying to work them out. You can't glue things back together. You have to wait for them to knit." The new year brought a new beginning, a time to heal and a time to wait for things to knit.

{ 12 }
A New Beginning

The belated trip to Hawaii, a year overdue, was planned as a second honeymoon. Within two weeks of the Tex Feldman party, the Brinkmans were boarding a plane at the L.A. International Airport, bound for Honolulu, with Paul pondering to the press, "maybe we'll continue on to the Orient." With her husband on her arm at their first post-reconciliation public appearance, Jeanne explained lightheartedly: "He's an old friend." Being such a high-profile celebrity couple, who seemed to be so perfect for one another before the break-up, the general feeling was hope for their future. "Jeanne and Paul really are going to patch things up," a close friend of Crain's confided to the press. "How long it will last is anybody's guess, because Paul is very jealous and hotheaded and a lot has happened that Jeanne won't easily forget, but Paul now seems to realize how much he loves her so everybody is hoping for the best."

The couple returned home to find their house in the Hollywood Hills had been robbed. It was the third burglary in as many weeks. Jeanne reported that a chair and desk, valued at $380, were taken between January 17 and 22. On December 27, days before their reconciliation, rifles and shotguns valued at $3,000 were reported stolen, as well as four pistols from an earlier burglary. Three weeks later, on Valentine's Day, Paul was back in court to face the assault and battery charges from the Christmas night brawl with Rhoads and Timothy Ryan. He denied assaulting the latter, instead claiming that Ryan tried to run him down with his car. Brinkman was cleared of the charges by a jury of six men and six women. Rhoads had told police at the time that Brinkman also hit him, but the manufacturer refused to sign a complaint.

If Jeanne's private life was moving along at a breakneck pace, her career had become lackluster. *The Tattered Dress* was released in March 1957. It was a standard programmer, which was interesting, but forgettable. She played the beleaguered wife of a high-profile attorney (portrayed by Universal heartthrob Jeff Chandler), but had very little to do. The *New York Times* review of the film summed up her contribution to the picture when it said: "Jeanne Crain is decorative too as the estranged but loving wife of our hero." Except for the estranged part, it could have been an excerpt from the review for *The Fastest Gun Alive*. She had made a couple of television appearances as herself on Bob Hope's show, as well as on Ed Sullivan. Those, combined with two roles in anthology programs, comprised her TV work before the divorce, which had drained her physically and emotionally. She was announced for the female lead in a thriller called *The Whole Truth*, which was being made in England in the late summer.

Paul's business had taken a different route as well. Just as Jeanne was filing her original divorce complaint the previous spring, Brinkman sold his manufacturing facility on North La Brea Avenue. Later in the year he purchased a controlling share in the Port Lumber company, a wholesale lumber distribution yard located at Port Hueneme in Ventura county. One of the assets acquired in this deal was a 51-food yawl, christened the *Pavane*, which became a favorite pastime for Paul, who would take the entire family out for

The Brinkmans with their
North Roxbury neighbors, Lucille Ball and Desi Arnaz
(Courtesy of the Jeanne Crain Brinkman Family Trust)

regular boating jaunts.

In June, Jeanne announced that she was expecting her fifth child in November, and while she was between pictures, she and Paul decided to take the whole Brinkman clan aboard the *Pavane* for a "second honeymoon" cruise. On Monday, June 24, they set out from Newport Beach making their way toward Catalina Island, where the vessel ran aground. Paul managed to free the boat from the rocks and began heading back to Newport, when the *Pavane* developed a leak, which flooded the motor. The craft drifted for four hours in the heavy waters of the Catalina Channel, while Brinkman sent SOS calls on the yacht's radio and the hull took on more water.

Worthington Lee, a Corona del Mar contractor, picked up the distress call on his shortwave radio set. Lee also happened to be a vice-captain with the Coast Guard auxiliary, and notified Coast Guard officials at Newport Beach. A cutter was dispatched for rescue and the *Pavane* was sighted drifting toward the rocks of the rugged Newport jetty when it was taken in tow. Lee, who was along on the rescue said, "another thirty minutes and the yacht would have been smashed against the rocks." Paul later described the ordeal. "We were in danger of running aground several times," he explained, "and we were all seasick. The boat had sprung a leak and we had to do some fast bailing."

The lumber company had been a good investment for Brinkman. As a wholesale distributor, it sold to retail distribution outlets in the coastal counties surrounding the port, and it had steadily increased its volume since Paul had taken the reins. In August, however, there was a clash over questions of business ethics between Paul, as the owner of the lumber lease on Dock 1, a prime location at the Port Hueneme harbor, and Earney Thompson, a commissioner of the Oxnard Harbor District. Thompson charged Brinkman with selling lumber on both a wholesale and a retail level, a violation of the ethics of the business. "You have violated your contract 100 percent," the commissioner told Paul, as the two faced off over a meeting room table. Brinkman interpreted the charge as "direct slander." "I have never had my ethics questioned before," he declared, insisting that he did not believe there was any ground for cancelling his lease.

Thompson, a lumber retailer in Oxnard, told commissioners that the district was being criticized "all over the county for the operation that is going on here," and that the Port Lumber Company was using subterfuge to conceal retail transactions. "As long as I get paid, what's the difference?" Brinkman replied. Cancelation of his lease was an option because according to its conditions, he had to apply for renewal a month in advance of its expiration. The commission investigated the matter and later the same week, the Port Lumber Company's lease was canceled, despite Brinkman's pleading with the panel.

The lumber company issue wasn't the only one Paul dealt with during the late summer. The week before the ethics charges were brought forth, Brinkman settled out of court, a $50,000 damage suit brought against him by a seventy-year-old widow. Anna Purcell claimed she was struck and injured by an automobile driven by Brinkman as she crossed a Beverly Hills intersection in early 1956. The case had been scheduled for trial on August 20, but was settled the following day with an undisclosed amount of money. The week after the Port Lumber Company incident, a $95,000 damage suit was filed against both Paul and Jeanne by Timothy Ryan, friend of Homer Rhoads. Although his complaint offered no details, it was in response to the Christmas day fight between he, Paul and Rhoads, and claimed he was beaten by Brinkman and suffered permanent damage to his eye as a result.

With her baby due in the fall, Jeanne had to withdraw from the British film, *The Whole Truth*. It was the first time she missed out on a picture due to pregnancy since her days at Twentieth Century-Fox. Always wanting a large family, and the new baby a product of her reconciliation with Paul, it was an easy price to pay. On Thursday, November 21, Jeanne gave birth to her fifth child at the Queen of Angels Hospital. It was another little girl and her parents named her Lisabette Ann, Betsy to her family. The doctor let Jeanne come home two days early to eat Thanksgiving dinner with Paul and the children.

Within a month of Lisabette's birth, Louella Parsons announced that Jeanne had signed on to play the female lead in *Guestward Ho!*, a television series that was being developed by CBS. Based on a 1956 memoir by Patrick Dennis, famous for penning *Auntie Mame*, *Guestward Ho!* was the story of a New York ad-executive and his wife who move to New Mexico to run a dude ranch. A month later, a start time for the pilot still had yet to be scheduled. Paul, who was set to produce the series, said he wanted Jeanne "to rest up after the birth of the baby." When asked if he would have a role in the potential show, the former actor replied, "Certainly not. I still remember how hammy I was." Although the series was still on tap in early March 1958, it never materialized and CBS dropped its option. *Guestward Ho!* did finally make it to network television during the 1960-61 season on ABC, and starred Joanne Dru.

Brinkman's legal woes continued, when on Wednesday, March 19, he was booked at the West Los Angeles jail on a charge of interfering with an officer. According to C.E. Klingler, the motorcycle cop whose beat was in the neighborhood of Paul's manufacturing office, he was ticketing Brinkman's car for double parking outside the office

Paul and Jeanne at the Long Island estate of
aviation magnate, Sherman Fairchild
(Courtesy of the Jeanne Crain Brinkman Family Trust)

when Paul grabbed his arm and protested that another automobile was parked in his driveway.

Klingler instructed him to wait until he was finished writing a ticket for another vehicle, but Brinkman held tight to his arm. When the officer broke free from his grip, the irate businessman yelled: "You struck me. I've got twenty witnesses. Take your hands off me." Klingler then put him under arrest, when Brinkman retorted: "I'll have your job for this. I want you to know I'm a good friend of the police chief. I've never been manhandled before and no punk like you is going to get away with this." He was later released on $500 bail, pleaded innocent and requested a court trial. In June, a municipal judge found him innocent of the charge.

On the same day of Paul's arrest, Universal Pictures Company, Inc. filed suit against Jeanne to recover $6,633.78 it lost when she became pregnant the previous year, before the expiration of her five-year contract. A month later, Crain demanded $30,288.30 from the studio in a counter-suit filed in Superior Court. She denied that she had been overpaid when she was unable to report for a film due to pregnancy, and demanded back-pay accrued since her last check on August 15, 1957.

As she approached thirty-three, Jeanne's big box-office days were behind her, despite still being a beauty. With a growing family, her time was suited to a full home life. "[The children] make a lot of commotion," she said, "and they take a lot of time, even with good help, but when you come home from the studio, after a particularly bad day, there is nothing in this world like five children to make you forget your problems." Still, she wanted to act. Like many motion picture stars whose heyday was a decade earlier, she turned to television. In June 1958, she appeared in one of TV's early live productions of a classic novel, *The Great Gatsby*. F. Scott Fitzgerald's famed story had been filmed only once before, in 1949, at Paramount. For the television version, Jeanne played Daisy, the object of affection and obsession of Jay Gatsby, played by Robert Ryan. A *Playhouse 90* presentation on the CBS network, *Gatsby* was the live-TV debut for both Crain and Ryan. Live performance was something the film actress was not used to. "The whole thing got to me," she confessed. "They kept saying, 'Now don't worry, it'll all fall in place.' But it kept getting worse... I was in a black Irish mood. But, lo and behold, it did fall into place."

In October, she costarred in another small screen drama with Adam Kennedy and George Macready in "The Trouble with Ruth," on the *Schlitz Playhouse*. It was the story of a master criminal who discovers a kleptomaniac and threatens to tell her husband about it if she will not be his accomplice in a daring robbery scheme. As the kleptomaniac, Jeanne threw herself into the role and was frightened by the impulses she felt while preparing for the part. "Since I'd never known a kleptomaniac," she explained, "I had to do research. I deliberately wandered through a chic jewelry shop in Beverly Hills, looking at the beautiful things on display. I tried to figure out what compulsion would motivate me to steal." It may have been an exercise in acting research but it did little to increase her standing after more than a year away from the big screen.

After the new year, she was signed for an all-star special to be produced for CBS. *Meet Me in St. Louis*, the much-loved MGM musical starring Judy Garland, was adapted for television and featured Jeanne as Rose, the eldest sister of the Smith family. The high-profile cast included Myrna Loy (with whom she had worked so well on the two *Cheaper by the Dozen* movies) as well as Jane Powell, Walter Pidgeon, Ed Wynn and child-actress Patty Duke. With the program set to premiere on April 26, the troupe rehearsed for several weeks on Second Avenue in New York City, and Jeanne promoted the two-hour special on the popular TV game shows, *I've Got a Secret* and *What's My Line?* The reviews for the live presentation were relatively positive, though Crain's notices were rather mediocre. *Billboard's* observation that her performance was "more than capable" was a far cry from the glowing words bestowed during her glory days at Fox. She did, however, enjoy the less hectic schedule of occasional television roles in comparison to the rigorous hours at a studio. "This is the kind of life we used to dream about," she said. "We all hoped for a time when we could freelance for parts, shop around and do only what we liked. And have some time to travel. And still make a decent living. And this I have."

The week after *Meet Me in St. Louis* aired, Jeanne began shooting her first feature film since *The Joker is Wild*, three years earlier. It was a western called *Guns of the Timberland* and costarred Alan Ladd, with whom Jeanne had never made a picture. Produced by Warner Brothers and based on a Louis L'Amour novel, it was the story of the struggle between ranchers and lumbermen, with Jeanne playing a lady-rancher. In addition to playing the male lead, Ladd was the film's executive producer and had high hopes for the picture to be a sprawling success. He cast teen singing idol Frankie Avalon in his acting debut (before he hit the beach with Annette Funicello) and his own daughter and namesake, Alana Ladd, in a featured role as Avalon's love interest. The movie was shot on location in Nevada and Northern California and when she wrapped filming, Jeanne appeared in a couple more television projects later in the year. When released, *Guns of the Timberland* proved to be "routine fare strictly for the action market," and the movie did little to revive a career that had become mediocre. "No matter how long you're in this business," Jeanne told reporters, "you can't take some time off without people thinking something has happened. If you allow your name to get out of circulation, it doesn't mean as much. It's a phenomenon." Though she continued to work, she couldn't regain the career momentum exhibited before her divorce proceedings. Whether it was the constant negative press resulting from the incident, or the public's lack of acceptance for a more glamorous and sophisticated Jeanne Crain, the results were less than stellar.

At the end of September, the Brinkmans announced that their sixth child was expected in January. When the time came, Jeanne was taken to the Queen of Angels Hospital, and on Sunday, January 10, 1960, Maria Josepha was born. She weighed five pounds, 8 ¼ ounces and evened out the Brinkman brood to three boys and three girls. Their ever-growing family didn't hinder the couple's active social life. By the late '50s and early '60s, Jeanne and Paul were considered part of Hollywood's Café Society, the "hard core of fun-seekers" among celebrities. This group made its way to big movie premieres, publicity cocktail parties and banquets, and along with the Brinkmans, included Jayne Mansfield and Mickey Hargitay, Zsa Zsa Gabor, Esther Williams and Jeff Chandler, the Robert Stacks, Dorothy Malone and Joan Collins, among others. Fulfilling one of their dreams as newlyweds, they traveled extensively, and were often members of Conrad Hilton's entourage. Along with other celebrities, they would join the famed hotelier in opening new properties around the globe, including his posh Nile Hilton in Cairo, Egypt in 1959. Their social activities crossed over into the political arena as well.

When Jeanne was a child, her parents were registered Republicans. When they divorced, Loretta registered as a Democrat, following in the footsteps of her own parents' politics. Before World War II ended, however, the single mother had reverted back to her Republican standing at the polls. Both Jeanne and Paul were registered Republicans and campaigned heavily for the Eisenhower-Nixon ticket in 1952.

As part of the Entertainment Industry Joint Committee for Eisenhower-Nixon, Crain engaged in "the first political campaigning of her life," speaking, along with Hedda Hopper, at a women's event called "Coffee Hour for Eisenhower." The purpose of the committee was to raise money and provide entertainment for Republican programs. Such was her task when she headed the entertainment portion of a Nixon rally in Los Angeles just days before the election. Other prominent Hollywood stars who campaigned for the ticket included Irene Dunne, Lucille Ball and Dick Powell.

When Eisenhower's two terms were complete in 1960, Jeanne was part of the large group of Hollywood celebrities in the Nixon camp, "fighting for the GOP cause" against John F. Kennedy. When that presidential run was unsuccessful, Nixon made a bid in the California governor's race during the 1962 campaign cycle and Crain, along with fellow stars, John Payne, Ginger Rogers and Cesar Romero, backed him once again, appearing on a pre-election telethon.

While campaigning for Nixon in 1960, Timothy Ryan's battery suit finally made it to trial. Jeanne had to testify regarding the Christmas day fight between Ryan and her husband. When asked if she ever had illicit relations with Homer Rhoads, Crain emphatically denied that she had. A reluctant witness, Jeanne was technically summoned into court to help Ryan's case, but her testimony was clearly in her husband's favor. The following day, after nearly four years, it took a jury of ten women and two men only three hours to finally award Ryan $5,000 of the $95,000 he was seeking. "I am very much surprised at this verdict," Paul

The Brinkman Family in 1960
(Standing, l-r) Michael, Paul, Paul, Jr. (Seated, l-r)
Timothy, Lisabette, Jeanne, holding Maria, and Jeanine
(Courtesy of the Jeanne Crain Brinkman Family Trust)

remarked. His attorney, Robert Nye, claimed they would ask for a new trial. The whole incident left other emotional casualties, with Homer and Hilda Rhoads finalizing their own high stakes divorce six months later.

After the election and her time in court, Jeanne entered a whirlwind period of filming, with two new movie projects for American companies and plans being finalized for pictures to be made in Italy. She closed a deal to co-star with former fellow Fox alum, Victor Mature, in *The Trojan War*, to be shot in Rome. She and Paul were scheduled to sail from New York to Italy on board the *Liberte* in mid-October. Plans were laid for Jeanne to be on location in Rome for the rest of the year. Italian bombshell Gina Lollobrigida offered the Brinkmans the loan of her villa, a dwelling large enough to house their whole family during the Christmas holidays, when the children would fly over to be with their parents. Too many delays on the script, however, forced both Mature and Crain to bow out of the Italian epic.

Instead, Jeanne signed with Italian producer Octavio Poggi to play Nefertiti in *The Lonely Queen*, co-starring with Vincent Price and Cliff Robertson (who ended up being replaced), with filming scheduled to begin in Rome in spring 1961. "Sword-and-sandal" spectacles were all the rage during the late 1950s and early '60s, when Italian-made costume dramas set in ancient Rome attempted to emulate the big-budget Biblical sagas produced in Hollywood. Italian producers could hire high-profile American or British stars (whose careers were often in decline) and combine their name value with much lower European production costs to create an impressive, if forgettable, motion picture product.

In addition to her proposed European shoot, Jeanne returned to her old stomping grounds at Twentieth Century-Fox in November 1960. Her former Fox co-star, Dana Andrews, had purchased the rights to a novel called *The Build-Up Boys* about the cutthroat world of New York

Jeanne on her first trip to her beloved Rome in 1953
(Courtesy of the Jeanne Crain Brinkman Family Trust)

advertising. His intentions of selling the story to a studio for film production didn't pan out until Fox finally agreed to buy it. They changed the title to *Madison Avenue*, and cast Andrews in the lead, reuniting him with Crain and adding Eleanor Parker to bolster the star power. The roles played by Crain and Parker were turned down by Fox starlets, Suzy Parker and Joan Collins. Happy to take on the character, Jeanne exclaimed, "It's an excellent role. I think it's a mistake for actresses to turn down parts early in their careers. The way to get ahead is to act. Actors aren't actors unless they're acting." Andrews was now in his early fifties and *Madison Avenue* would be the last time he played a significant romantic leading man. By Hollywood standards, Crain and Parker were approaching middle age and the film's appeal was limited to a nostalgic audience.

After the new year, Jeanne had another acting gig for television, but this time it was a pilot for her own show. Tentatively titled *Love & Kisses*, the show was a comedy, produced by Tony Owen, the then-husband of actress Donna Reed, whose own popular TV program Owen produced. *Love & Kisses* became *The Jeanne Crain Show* and had its star playing a former top model, while John Vivyan appeared as her husband and editor of a high fashion magazine. The pilot for the sophisticated situation comedy was completed by mid-February, 1961, and was not alone as a showcase for big-name talent whose star had dimmed. The roster of potential situation comedies was filled with former studio all-stars including Jack Carson, Ginger Rogers, Phil Harris and his wife, Alice Faye, whose last screen musical, *The Gang's All Here*, saw Jeanne's film debut. The same season, Twentieth Century-Fox television was adapting Crain's 1946 hit, *Margie*, for the small screen as well. *The Jeanne Crain Show* was eventually aired as *His Model Wife*, but according to one observer the show "never had a chance," due to Crain's overpowering glamour. In his syndicated column, reviewer Rick Du Brow wrote:

> "Miss Crain is simply too much of a dish. There is more money in being folksy on television. Potential women customers must never feel the pangs of envy or jealousy... The fact that the program wasn't funny really isn't too important,

as most of our successful domestic comedies have proved. More harmful, from a commercial point of view, were Miss Crain's plunging neckline and well-kept figure, which were enough to make many a less-preserved housewife flip the dial."

In late January 1961, Jeanne signed on for *Twenty Plus Two*, a detective caper which costarred David Janssen, who was just coming off his own TV series, *Richard Diamond, Private Detective*. The film, described as a "weak contrived murder mystery," felt like an extended episode of a television whodunit, and when filming wrapped in March, Crain finally made the trip to Rome to shoot *The Lonely Queen*, which was retitled *Nefertiti, Queen of the Nile*.

She took Loretta and her eldest daughter, nine-year-old Jeanine, with her. While there, the three lived on the top floor of a quaint Italian hotel, and Jeanne placed Jeanine in an Italian-speaking Catholic school. Loretta and her granddaughter would sometimes visit Jeanne on the film set, but most often, Mrs. Crain would pick the young girl up after school and take her to an English tea house, where they would eat sandwiches and Jeanine would practice manners. Despite her love for Italy, after spending most of the summer there, Jeanne longed for home. "I like to keep working," she told a reporter, "but I'd rather do it in the United States. I have a break between pictures, so I'll have time for a short visit to Southern California before returning to Rome." Instead of traveling back to the States, however, she attended the Berlin Film Festival, then returned to Rome to complete her second Italian feature, *Pontius Pilate*. The film was another Biblical epic and cast Jeanne as Claudia, the wife of

Pilate (played by French matinee idol, Jean Marais), who condemned Christ to death.

After a short trip home, Crain returned to Italy in late September to star in *With Iron and Fire*, a historical spectacle set in 17th-century Ukraine, and based on a novel by Henryk Sienkiewicz, the author of *Quo Vadis*. Paul joined her in Rome, this time, leaving the children with Loretta. Jeanne and her *Nefertiti* co-star, Vincent Price, were good friends and fellow art lovers. They were both at Fox in the '40s and appeared together in *Leave Her to Heaven*. While on location, Paul and Vincent would scour the flea markets in Rome, and Price took Crain on a shopping spree for local paintings. The veteran actor would later joke about this period in his career: "I made some dreadful pictures in Italy. They were terrible. But I bought so much good art." Jeanne came home with eight "gorgeous paintings" of her own, and went back to pick up the Italian version of the Oscar for her portrayal of Nefertiti.

The quality of her recent movies was reflected in how slowly they were released to American audiences. Of the five pictures made within a twelve-month span, only one, *Twenty Plus Two*, was seen in the United States within months of completed filming. Shooting wrapped on *Madison Avenue* in November 1960, but it didn't make it to the screen until 1962. Her Italian epics lingered on studio shelves even longer. *Nefertiti, Queen of the Nile* didn't make its American debut until 1964, and *With Iron and Fire*, the following year. (The latter film also went by the titles, *Invasion 1700* and *Daggers of Blood*, potentially confusing the small audience that might be interested) *Pontius Pilate* was the last to be released, in 1967, a full six years after its completion. When she returned to the United States, Jeanne continued to do some television work, but her days as a significant leading lady were over.

{ 13 }
The Family Brinkman (and Crain)

After she returned home from Italy, Jeanne's film projects became few and far between. Instead, she turned her focus toward television, appearing in a handful of dramatic programs. In March 1962, she costarred with Ronald Reagan in the *General Electric Theater* presentation, "My Dark Days," a two-part story about Marion Miller, an American housewife who served as an undercover agent for the FBI to expose Communist activities. It was the first time she had ever had the opportunity to meet a person she played on the screen. "This woman did a tremendous job for her country," the star said, "and is still paying for it. She is constantly harassed by Communist lovers." After two more small screen appearances, she transitioned to the stage, at the insistence of her mother. Always in the background, Loretta could see that her daughter's film offers were coming less than they once were, and to keep Jeanne's name in the public eye, she persuaded her to work in summer stock theater.

The Philadelphia Story had been a smash hit on Broadway in 1939, with Katharine Hepburn making famous the leading role of Tracy Lord. Its film adaption the following year was Hepburn's great movie comeback from the brink of "box-office poison." In the summer of 1963, Jeanne signed on to play the part at Chicago's Drury Lane Theater, an entertainment landmark in the Windy City. It was an exciting time, and when she arrived in town for the show's rehearsals, she garnered ohhs and ahhs from the whole cast, who thought the mother of six was stunning. Paul remained on the west coast, but Loretta accompanied her daughter, as she would during her future touring engagements.

On Monday night, September 2, Crain made her stage debut, in what turned out to be a rousing success, with the last two weeks of the show sold out. The Drury's box-office claimed its heaviest ticket demand of the season, and Jeanne took the show on tour, giving performances in Milwaukee and Atlanta. If her four-week run on the Chicago stage showed promise, her contention for leading roles in two television series, *Please Don't Eat the Daisies* and *Peyton Place*, didn't pan out, with the parts going to other actresses. The following spring, she was back at the Drury in *Claudia*, and another summer stock road trip ensued, which included stops in Pennsylvania, New Jersey and New York.

During Christmas week 1964, Jeanne told Hedda Hopper that "actresses can't win," when MGM wanted to cast her as the mother in *Meet Me in St. Louis*, a potential half-hour television pilot for ABC. The network nixed the idea, stating she wasn't the motherly type and the public wouldn't accept her as such. As the mother of six, Crain was frustrated by this assumption, and to add to the mix she was expecting her seventh child the following May. "I'm told the seventh child is apt to be extraordinary," Jeanne exclaimed. "This one may be born on my birthday." When spring rolled in, her clairvoyance proved true, and on May 25, her fortieth birthday, she welcomed her seventh child at St. John's Hospital in Santa Monica. The baby was a boy, who was named Christopher. Jeanne told a reporter that she and Paul

Jeanne and the cast of *The Philadelphia Story* at the
Drury Lane Theatre in Chicago, 1963
(Courtesy of the Jeanne Crain Brinkman Family Trust)

took the jokes in stride about their ever-growing family. "People say 'Are you playing Vatican roulette' or 'Are you Catholic or careless'," she explained. With the large family, and Jeanne's extensive schedule away from home, the Brinkmans employed a couple who had helped manage the household for over a decade. "They've been with us since before the three youngest children were born," the actress said, "so they're really part of the family. Also, the older children take care of the younger ones, and two of the boys can drive, so it's no problem for Paul and me to get away."

By the mid '60s, Jeanne's name was turning up in question and answer columns with fans asking what had happened to her. With no career opportunities of substance to report at that time, the answers generally revolved around her large family. "I love both my children and my profession and I have always prided myself on neglecting neither," she proclaimed. She did indeed love every one of her children deeply, and according to her daughter, Lisabette, "would never allow any of us to 'rat' on one of our siblings; it was against her principles. She told us it was more important to her that we be close to each other than to try to gain favor with her!"

When her older children were born, (referred to within the family as the "big 4"), and her career was running high, Jeanne spent most of her time working. Long days on the movie set would often begin at 5 a.m. and run late into the evening. In contrast, she wanted to spend more hands-on time with her second group of children, born after she and Paul reconciled in 1957. As an avid reader and book collector, Crain instilled her love of books to her offspring, and trips to the bookstore (and art supply store) were special treats. When Lisabette and Maria were small, she would read with them regularly at night. After delving into the Dr. Doolittle series, the trio would then forge ahead into all the Dr. Seuss collection, topping off the experience with a visit to UCLA to meet the colorful doctor himself (aka Theodor Geisel).

Unlike the formality and rigidness of some Hollywood domiciles, the Brinkmans were a normal family; a big, chaotic household, where Saturdays held pony rides and lunch at the Farmer's Market. Paul would take the two youngest girls with him to watch his tennis matches every weekend. During California heat waves, all the kids would drag their mattresses out by the swimming pool to sleep. Summers were spent at their house in Emerald Bay at Laguna Beach, where Crain had got her start with photographer William Mortensen, twenty plus years before. Hours were spent taking long walks along the beach, collecting shells, swimming and sunbathing, with Jeanne contentedly lost in one of her books under an umbrella, wearing her favorite old straw hat.

Jeanne with her seventh and last child, Christopher,
who was born on her 40th birthday, 1965
(Courtesy of the Jeanne Crain Brinkman Family Trust)

Her first role after Christopher's birth was another TV pilot called *Men Against Evil*, which costarred Howard Duff. It was a cop show and Jeanne described it as "kind of 'Dragnet' or 'Naked City,' with the accent on what happens to the policemen after they finish their daily routine." She played the wife of Duff's character, a veteran lieutenant on the force. *Men Against Evil* put emphasis on the cops' home lives, aiming to be a *Peyton Place* for the men-in-blue set, but after the pilot aired, Jeanne was dropped, and the show's title was changed to *The Felony Squad*. "I liked the idea [of showcasing the cops' personal lives]," Duff confessed, "but when we saw the pilot we all knew it wouldn't work."

With the television show defunct, Jeanne signed on as the adult female lead in a picture called *Hot Rods to Hell*. Her co-star for the fourth and final time was Dana Andrews. It had been twenty-one years since their first pairing in *State Fair* and a lot of proverbial water had gone under the bridge. Andrews had struggles with alcohol and it showed. At forty-one, Jeanne was still lovely of face and figure, though her over-the-top performance was noted by many. The movie centered around Andrews' character, Tom Phillips, his wife Peg (Crain) and their two teenaged children, all of whom initially live in Boston. When Tom hurts his back in an automobile accident, he can no longer work as a traveling salesman, so he takes his family across country to run a motel in the California desert. En route they are taunted and tormented by a group of thrill-seeking teens in hot rods on a desert highway, and the wild youngsters continue their disrespectful antics when Phillips arrives at the motel.

The B-picture was based on a *Saturday Evening Post* story from the 1950s and originally intended for television under the title *52 Miles to Terror*. In the "so-bad-its-good" category of campy '60s films, the picture bore such taglines as: "They're souped up for thrills and there's no limit to what they'll do!" and "Hotter than Hell's Angels! The motorcycle gangs take a back seat, when these young animals clear the road for excitement!" It was the last movie by veteran director John Brahm, who made the dark thrillers, *The Lodger* and *Hangover Square* at Fox during the mid-1940s, when Crain and Andrews were in their heyday. With the acting and directing trio producing a product which would have done better a decade earlier, one critic hit the mark when he observed: "Given the year of its making, *Hot Rods to Hell* may represent one of the last times that the aging, pre-boomer generation got to have its cranky say in a movie industry that would shut out most voices over forty."

When it was released in early 1967, critics weren't kind, though under the circumstances they weren't expected to be. "Both Andrews and Miss Crain, whose stars once shone brightly, ham it up in a most unconvincingly, preacherly way," penned a reviewer who reflected the general consensus. Indeed, when Jeanne signed on to make the movie, it still bore its original title and she wasn't happy about the name change, remarking, "Frankly, I wouldn't go to a picture named *Hot Rods to Hell*." She felt that with the current state of motion pictures, there weren't good parts for "a wholesome, middle-aged screen queen." She turned down the part of a mother who has a passionate love affair with her son's eighteen-year-old friend. "I have *sons* that age," she said. "I know I may sound resentful," she continued, "but it seems to me that Elizabeth Taylor and Audrey Hepburn get all the good parts these days."

Indeed, her oldest sons were grown and, in 1969, Michael was the first of her children to marry, and Paul, Jr. was in college. With more time to devote to painting, Jeanne, who began taking art courses at UCLA a few years earlier, expanded to private classes. Ever on the quest to improve her artistic abilities, she began studying with painter Arnold Schifrin. The artist would hold painting sessions with models at his studio in West Los Angeles, and Jeanne would attend these classes a couple of times a week when she wasn't filming or away doing stage work. Having sold their house in Beverly Hills in the early '60s, the Brinkmans bought a home on Hilgard Avenue in the Westwood section of Los Angeles, near the university, as well as the house in Laguna Beach. Jeanne became a member of the Westwood Art Association, and a student at the Laguna School of Art and Design. She had a painting studio in the house at Hilgard and she would bring home what she was working on in class for Paul to critique. He respected her talent and love of art and when she was pregnant with her last child, Christopher, and couldn't paint with her beloved oils due to the toxicity, the couple took a sculpture class together at UCLA.

Crain joined a group of local artists, led by Schifrin, on a painting trip to Florence, Italy, where the troupe settled in at the Villa Villoresi, an elegant, centuries old palazzo, near the city. Upon their return to the States, the association hosted an exhibit displaying the work created by its members during the Italian tour, including Jeanne's. She had fallen in love with Italy since her first visit after completing *Duel in the Jungle* in 1953. Her deep bond with the country only

Jeanne and Lisabette, 1970
(Courtesy of the Jeanne Crain Brinkman Family Trust)

increased after making films there in the early '60s. "Mortgage the house, sell the car, anything to go back to Italy," she would proclaim, and in 1969, with the four eldest children grown (or practically so; Jeanine was seventeen), she and Paul seriously contemplated moving there with the three youngest.

    While studying at Schifrin's studio, she met Julon Moser, a watercolorist who had studied at the Chouinard Art Institute with painter Millard Sheets, and was esteemed throughout California. She and Jeanne became great friends, and along with another artist, formed their own painting society of three, making trips to Europe and Mexico together to paint. She thrived on the camaraderie of these and other friendships she culled within the artist community, and her creative spirit would blossom on these trips. Although oils were her passion, Crain loved to experiment with new and different media.

As the 1970s began, the actress held many irons in the fire. In addition to her art endeavors, Crain also continued to appear on the theater circuit, which included more travel. In May, 1970, she played three weeks at the Pheasant Run Playhouse in St. Charles, Illinois, in *Janus*, a romantic comedy which had a run on Broadway in the mid- 1950s starring Margaret Sullavan. She graced TV talk shows and became the national representative for the Toni Company, a beauty firm for which she made several television commercials. She also lent her name to a clothing line, Jeanne Crain of Hollywood, which was advertised in popular ladies' periodicals across the country. Privately, she continued to enjoy the company of other actresses of her era as part of a Beverly Hills sewing circle called the "Sew & Sews," a group of which she had been a member for years (The "Sew and Sew Club" was even mentioned in a magazine advertisement for Kenmore sewing machines, in which Crain appeared with Christopher in 1970).

In 1971, Jeanne signed on for a film role, her first since *Hot Rods to Hell*. The movie was called *Whispers in the Dark* and was to be directed by Lee Madden, who had just enjoyed success with two low-budget action flicks, *Hell's Angels, '69* and *Angel Unchained*. Jeanne was cast as the middle-aged wife of a murdered minister (he was crucified at the base of his pulpit!). Her character, Fanny, is then stalked and terrorized by the same Charles Manson-like cult crazies who killed her husband. The film came on the cusp of the frenzied media mania of the Manson killings and featured a look-alike of the long-haired cult leader.

One review summed up the shenanigans when it said: "It's a lowbrow variation on *The Straw Dogs*, with Miss Crane [sic] and four teenagers in a house under siege by members of a pseudoreligious dope cult." The reviewer went on to offer sympathy to Jeanne. "There's nothing shameful about her performance, but it's sad to see her reduced to working in such a hokey little piece of junk." When *Whispers in the Dark* didn't do justice to the film's exploitation status, the title was changed to *The Night God Screamed*. Although it was shot and produced in 1971, distribution was intermittent in various markets through 1974, by Cinemation Industries, the same company who released films called *Shanty Tramp*, *The Sadist* and *I Drink Your Blood*. The feature showed up in small neighborhood theaters and drive-ins on a double bill with *The Horrible House on the Hill*, which cemented its place with a cult following.

On New Year's Day, 1972, it was announced that Jeanne had signed on to be part of an all-star cast in a disaster film called *Airborne*. With the enormous success of the mega-star airplane drama, *Airport*, MGM wanted to duplicate the magic with their own version, which they retitled, *Skyjacked*. Hoping to jumpstart her career, Jeanne drove herself through the main gate at MGM each day of shooting, ready to get back in the motion picture groove. As one of the many passengers, a middle-aged housewife whose husband is going through depression, she had little to do. "Someone decided it was time to bring Jeanne Crain out of retirement," chimed a *Skyjacked* reviewer, "so they toss her a few scant lines and let it go at that. She gets the billing and Ross Elliott, as her husband, gets the lumps." The picture was headed by square-jawed Charlton Heston and featured professional football player, Rosey Grier, and TV starlet Susan Day in their feature film debuts. It would be Jeanne's movie swan song. *Skyjacked*, along with an episode of *Owen Marshall, Counsellor at Law*, a Perry Mason-esque television drama, were the last times she acted before the camera for the small or big screen.

Paul and Jeanne at the Brown Derby, 1970
(Courtesy of the Jeanne Crain Brinkman Family Trust)

Though she had ceased acting in movies, Crain's next role was dramatic, nonetheless. Paul, Jr. was newly graduated from Southwestern University Law School, and Jeanne was urged to take part in a mock trial at a California State Bar convention in September of 1974. In front of hundreds of attorneys in Sacramento, Jeanne played "Cathy Cutie," a rape victim who was invited out for coffee by "Paul Playboy" after meeting him in a bar. According to the scenario, the couple drove to a local lover's lane, where Cathy claimed Paul Playboy raped her. Mr. Playboy contended that she consented. A San Diego lawyer played the defense attorney and Paul Brinkman, Sr. played Mr. Playboy.

The skit was in response to the state's new law regarding rape testimony and how then-current trial practices affected the victim. As the fictional defense attorney delved into 35-year-old Cutie's sexual history (going back as far as her high school prom), he attempted to prove that the alleged victim was in the habit of having sex with men on lover's lane. "It seemed quite offensive to have it brought out," exclaimed Jeanne. "I got very emotional about it. It seemed like even the district attorney was against me." The new law, which took effect the following January, would restrict testimony about a rape victim's prior sexual conduct.

In the late '60s, Paul took an interest in purchasing some ranch property, and bought land in the Sacramento River Valley, near Red Bluff in Northern California. He moved his horse and the children's ponies there, where they ran wild, with no foreman yet hired. The location proved problematic, being too far from Los Angeles for easy travel and a couple of years later, he acquired some 3,400 acres of the Salsipuedes Ranch near Lompoc, in Santa Barbara county, and later in Gaviota, a large, mostly undeveloped coastal property sandwiched between the Los Padres National Forest and the

Santa Barbara Channel. In December 1972, the Brinkmans applied to have the parcel near Lompoc placed into a preserve. Most of it was used for cattle, but other parts were used to grow dry beans and flower seed. The whole family would enjoy long weekends at Salsipuedes, with the three oldest Brinkman boys driving up for cattle round-ups, and Jeanne preparing large dishes of lasagna for the big shindig thrown by Paul for the riders and their families.

By the mid-1970s, Crain began settling into life off the screen. Her children were getting older and more independent. The first of her grandchildren were born and she enjoyed them on a regular basis, having them over on weekends and sometimes a week a at time. She continued to paint and be an active part of her local art community, with much of her work selling in local Los Angeles area shows. For years she took an annual retreat to the Monastery of the Angels with her good friend Ann Blyth and other Catholic ladies in the Hollywood community. She and Paul enjoyed regular games of backgammon, and her mother, Loretta, was still a big part of her life, now living in a house just a few blocks away from the Brinkman's Hilgard Avenue home. It had taken much energy to live in the limelight, to live such a full life for so many years in Hollywood, giving so much of herself to so many different people. She was ready to rest.

{ 14 }
An Armful of Babies or a Scrapbook Full of Screen Credits

1977 was an incredibly difficult year for Jeanne. Her family had always been an extremely important part of her life. She had always been close to her aunts, uncles and cousins from her mother's side of the family. In January, her cousin, Bob Rousseau, died tragically, at age fifty, while on a skiing vacation in Montana. A prominent radiologist, he was less than a year younger than Jeanne, and had been like a brother to her. The two had stayed in touch regularly throughout the years and his death devastated her. His mother, Marie, one of Loretta's sisters, passed away just five months later.

Then, in early September, Jeanne's sister, Rita, was the victim of a horrible house fire, and, like her cousin Bob Rousseau, was only fifty-years-old. Her body was found in the bedroom of her small, stucco home in West Los Angeles. Although she had been an enthusiastic woman, with a vibrant personality, Rita had lived her life in her famous sister's shadow. Since the Crain girls were young, Loretta's focus had been on Jeanne, even more so once she developed a career. While still in college, Rita worked as Jeanne's stand-in during the shooting of *Leave Her to Heaven*, and had "film ambitions of her own." After graduating from UCLA in the late 1940s, she tried unsuccessfully to follow in her sister's footsteps. She screen-tested at Twentieth Century-Fox, and even sat for William Mortensen, the man who helped launch her sister's career, sessions for which the photographer billed Jeanne. She became regularly involved in Junior League and Catholic charities, and in 1958, she married Vincent Holian, son of an old San Francisco family. She and Holian had a son, Kevin, and divorced after less than a decade together. Yet again, the comparisons of domestic life could be made with her successful sibling's long-term marriage and large family.

Rita and her son were an integral part of Jeanne's life and her children's. Paul felt the same antagonism toward his sister-in-law as he did for Loretta, but the younger Brinkmans enjoyed their aunt and she genuinely enjoyed them. When he was born, she was named Paul Jr.'s godmother and as he and the other children grew, she would take them on outings to the park or the movies, and on New Year's to the Rose Parade in Pasadena. Though she had suffered health problems since childhood, she was fun and lively, and was always invited to the big family dinners held at Jeanne's house every Sunday night, along with Loretta and Paul's mother, Gertrude. As well, Rita and Kevin would join her mother for the Brinkman's huge 4th of July beach celebration every summer, staying in a house Jeanne rented for them in downtown Laguna. Her health issues would only be complicated by a drinking problem, and though her sister tried to help her in any way she could, Rita's tragic death capped off what proved to be an unhappy life.

The devastation over her sister was compounded when three months later, the week before Christmas, Crain's father, George, died. His name had popped up in movie magazines on occasion during the '40s and '50s, when an article writer wanted to detail Jeanne's "idyllic" upbringing,

Rita and Jeanne at the Beverly Hills Hotel, 1958
(Courtesy of the Jeanne Crain Brinkman Family Trust)

Rita Marie Crain in the late 1940s by
photographer William Mortensen
(Courtesy of the Jeanne Crain Brinkman Family Trust)

but as his daughters grew older, under Loretta's influence, George saw less of them. When Rita married, both her engagement and wedding announcements claimed that her father's name was William B. Crain, and that he was deceased, a decision based on her mother's bitterness.

Jeanne's children had always been under the impression that their grandfather was indeed dead, until 1963, when Paul, Jr., then a sixteen-year-old student at Loyola High School, approached his mother about George. She told him that his grandfather was still living and in Los Angeles. The teen contacted him, and the two met one Saturday morning over coffee. Young Paul discovered that Mr. Crain had been retired from his job at Inglewood High School, and was currently working as an accountant for the Teamsters Union. On Christmas Eve, after Paul, Jr.'s initial meeting, Jeanine, answered a knock on the door to find her grandpa George standing on the other side. He introduced himself and asked if he could come in. He received a cool reception from Jeanne, who could never forget his leaving when she and Rita were young. He would, however, receive a regular invitation to the family's big Thanksgiving and Christmas dinners, where he would sit with a drink in his hand and chain-smoke cigarettes. By this time, he was a gentle, mild-mannered man, well-liked by his grandchildren.

George and Rita became closer as well, and he bought her a house, where the two lived together for a short period before he moved to a modest home in Canoga Park, in the San Fernando Valley. When his daughter died, George attended her funeral at St. Paul the Apostle Church, his grief obvious and heart-wrenching. Three months later, Paul, Jr., newly engaged, helped him move into a nursing home, a choice the elderly gentleman made himself. The next day, it was Paul, Jr. who received the call that his grandfather had suffered a massive heart attack and died that morning.

By the late '70s, Maria and Christopher were the only children still living at home, with Lisabette moving back in

George Crain at Inglewood High School, 1942

for short periods during and just after college. Jeanne's attention turned even more toward her aging mother. Besides buying Loretta the house she lived in on Warner Avenue, very near to her own home, Jeanne paid her a monthly stipend for all she had done for her. Loretta had literally lived for her oldest daughter, and held control over much of her life, managing her early career and becoming a constant figure in the lives of her family, as mother, grandmother and Jeanne's personal assistant. They were in contact almost daily, and for years had a standing Tuesday lunch date at Scandia restaurant on Sunset Boulevard, a longtime favorite of the Brinkmans. When they returned home from school on Tuesday afternoons, the children knew they would find their mother and grandmother on the living room sofa sipping brandy. Loretta instructed her grandchildren to never call her "grandmother," instead, preferring to be called "La-La." She often picked the younger children up from school, depositing them at their own home, as they were never invited to her own, making her house strange and mysterious to them.

In her seventies, Loretta suffered from hypertension and heart disease, and had breathing problems caused by pulmonary fibrosis. Her condition worsened and became so bad that she moved into the house on Hilgard Avenue, so that Jeanne could look after her. On Sunday evening, May 13, 1979, she died. Ever since the early years of their marriage, Mrs. Crain had been the source of many serious and contentious arguments between Jeanne and Paul. She and her son-in-law barely tolerated one another, and yet, when she lay for weeks dying in his house, Paul tended to her alongside Jeanne, bathing and feeding her when his wife didn't have the strength to do so.

Loretta's death hit Jeanne hard. She had lost both her parents within eighteen months. Free of the emotional and physical demands of her mother, and with Paul spending even more time at the ranch near Lompoc, she found herself alone. Once a grand and elegant social butterfly in Hollywood, she began to see less of her old friends. Emotional wounds that had never really been dealt with, regarding her father and her husband, began to come to the surface, with long hours now available to review and contemplate her life. Depression that started to take root as early as her forties, began to manifest and she started drinking. Cocktail hour martinis had always been a part of the Brinkmans' routine, but after Loretta's passing, Jeanne's drinking began to accelerate.

Despite its longevity, the Brinkman marriage could be tempestuous. Both were passionate and charismatic individuals, and they often approached things differently. Jeanne was an encouraging, nurturing parent. Paul believed in negative reinforcement. A notorious flirt, Paul was also a jealous husband, if he felt there was a reason to be. Jeanne always believed the best about the people she loved. She would dismiss her husband's insensitivity, explaining to her children that he didn't mean to be the way he was, that he was the imperfect product of an imperfect upbringing. Marriage to Paul for more than three decades had its challenges, and like many couples, in Hollywood or anywhere else, their fights could be epic.

If she had made mistakes in her own union, her sense of self wasn't one of them. She wanted to pass on what she had learned to the next generation. "Autonomy in a relationship is crucial," she told her daughter, Lisabette, before she married. Indeed, the Brinkmans had spent much time apart during their marriage, pursuing their own careers and interests. In addition to periods when Jeanne was on road tours for stage productions or on location, without Paul, shooting a film, she would often go by herself to their house in Laguna Beach to read and paint and rejuvenate. Brinkman, in turn, spent much time without his wife, on hunting trips and later, on his ranch.

Jeanne, 1980
(Courtesy of the Jeanne Crain Brinkman Family Trust)

By the spring of 1980, her drinking had become worse, and she entered a rehab facility in her beloved Laguna. After two months there, she returned home clear-headed and radiant. She was happy, reuniting with her old painting group, and enjoying a large art exhibition in Los Angeles later that year, as well as taking a short painting trip to Italy with a new group of painters. Back home, however, Paul's attendance of her family recovery meetings, an integral part of the process, slacked off, and he continued to enjoy his evening cocktails in her presence. After about a year, she gradually began to drink again.

In March 1983, after being off the screen for more than a decade, Jeanne agreed to be a presenter at the annual Academy Awards. She and her former Twentieth Century-Fox costar, Cornel Wilde, were scheduled to reunite and present the award for best make-up. As the show date drew near, however, Crain contacted the producer, Howard Koch, to cancel and was replaced by her *Gentlemen Marry Brunettes* costar, Jane Russell. She later regretting not taking part.

She continued to travel into her sixties, feeding her insatiable curiosity of the world and the people in it. She took trips with Paul, as well as taking tours to the Middle and Far East, which were organized by the Los Angeles County Museum of Art. But as they grew older, Paul began to spend the majority of his time at his ranches, and for the next two decades, the Brinkmans lived separately. With her children grown and leading their own lives, Jeanne became lonely. She had always been a devoted Catholic and for years went on at least one annual spiritual retreat, as well as being closely involved with a group of cloistered nuns in Hollywood. Divorce at this point wasn't an option. She began to withdraw from the world, spending her time, as she had in her youth, with her books. Paul, on the other hand, was still a very active participant in the world he had chosen, heavily engaged in the ranching communities north of Santa Barbara. At the age of seventy-two, he shifted his base to the ranch at Gaviota, where he built a house, while letting his Saulsipeudes foreman live at his home near Lompoc.

A Brinkman family photo, taken at Lisabette's wedding in March 1984. (l-r) Paul, Jeanne, Michael, Bret (Michael's daughter, standing in front of Jeanne), Debbie (Michael's wife), Jeanine, Marylou (Timothy's future wife), Lisabette, Timothy (behind Lisabette), Jamie Binstock, (the groom), whose hand is on Jeff (Michael's son), Paul, Jr., Christopher, Maria, Kevin Holian (Rita's son) and in the foreground, Erin and Lynne (Paul, Jr.'s daughters)
(Courtesy of the Jeanne Crain Brinkman Family Trust)

Tragedy hit the family in the spring of 1992, when Michael died of an overdose of alcohol at the age of forty-three. Mike was athletic, handsome and very charismatic. He had a successful career in the computer industry, yet he also had a serious drinking problem. His parents were devastated by his death, as was his whole family. Paul, rarely vulnerable to his feelings, could only deal with the situation by telling himself that his son was gone on a trip from which he would be back at some point. He couldn't face the reality of losing his son. Jeanne was severely grief-stricken, more so than her family had ever seen her. Michael died on the anniversary of Loretta's death.

Though her family was concerned about her self-imposed isolation, Jeanne could not be dissuaded. From her perspective, they didn't know all the pain she had experienced and closed herself off from their pleadings. Then, in 1995, when she turned seventy, and already in a certain degree of physical decline, her daughters decided that Jeanne would be better off living closer to them and their father, so she moved from the family home on Hilgard Avenue to Santa Barbara. Once she settled in there, her children would come up and bring their kids to see their grandmother on regular occasions. As great-grandchildren were born, they too would visit, and the proud matriarch enjoyed the precious time with her various offspring (In addition to her own progeny, Jeanne welcomed visits from Rita's son, Kevin, and his small daughter). Paul would stop by regularly, bringing her fruit from his orchard, relaying what he had been doing and discussing any news of old friends. She also still had numerous fans across the globe. Ever since she made *Home in Indiana*, Crain had received vast amounts of fan mail. Even during her later years, hordes of letters and photo requests were shipped to her house in Los Angeles, then later to her Santa Barbara home. Her daughter, Lisabette, assisted her with it, but it continued to pour in from all over the world, and was impossible to keep up with.

The pain of Mike's passing still lingered with his parents, who remained in a state of shock over it, even as time passed. In 1997, the nightmare was re-lived when their youngest child, Chris, died of a heroin overdose at the age of thirty-one. He had been in local grunge rock bands in the mid '80s, and became the first guitarist for the group, Jane's Addiction, in 1985, which he helped form with his boyhood friend, Eric Avery. Jeanne made her way through the ordeal, but the shock drew her even further into herself, a state in which she remained for the rest of her life.

She became very sedentary and a caregiver came to the house daily to help. She suffered from painful arthritis, for which she consumed large amounts of aspirin (Jeanne claimed to have "a cast iron stomach") and her lungs were weak from her childhood bout of pneumonia. While in her late sixties, chronic obstructive pulmonary disease (COPD) had set it. She would talk on the phone with her Carr cousins, but discouraged visits to her home. She continued to read and watch old films. Fortunately, alcohol was no longer a problem, and once she moved to Santa Barbara, Jeanne stopped drinking. On Christmas, when Paul would come for the big family dinner, they would sit and talk and have a drink together, but that was her only martini for the year. She never seemed to miss it. During her last years, she was confined to her bed, and her family would sit with her and discuss movies and her memories, both of which she relished sharing.

Paul, Jr., who by this time was working in the production end of the film and television industry, would visit his parents regularly at their respective homes. In April, 2003, Paul, Sr. turned eighty-five. Always a vibrant and active man, his health began to deteriorate and on Wednesday, October 1, he died. The Brinkman children who lived nearby went to their father's house as soon as they heard the news. Lisabette was in Italy, and when her brother called, she caught a flight to California the next morning. A funeral Mass was held on Monday morning at the chapel of the Santa Barbara mission, followed by a celebration of life reception at the Santa Barbara Yacht Club, where he had been an active member. Jeanne, in a state of shock, and with her own health incapacities, did not attend the funeral, remaining at her home with her caregiver. Later in the evening, her extended family, children, grandchildren and great-grandchildren, returned to her house and continued their father's wake with her.

Two months later, on the morning of December 3, Jeanne suffered a heart attack, shortly after waking. Her caregiver was unsure of what to do, and Lisabette, who was staying with her at the time, continued to rub her hands and arms, trying to coax her back to consciousness. When the doctor came to the house, he confirmed that she had, indeed, had a heart attack. Over the next few days, she continued to feel poorly and her blood pressure was dropping at an alarming rate. She was admitted to the hospital for testing, and on Sunday, December 7, while awaiting the results, Jeanne told Lisabette that she knew she was dying. The tests revealed the right chamber of her heart was enlarged and had a hole in it. The family was told she might have a few months at the most to live. She returned home two days later, under hospice care. She had no appetite for food and her system began to shut down. Family members came to say goodbye to her over the next few days, while her daughters stood vigil every night to make her as comfortable as they could. Always close to his mother, Paul, Jr. thanked her for what she had done for him, most notably for passing on to him her strong and devout Catholic faith. On Sunday morning, December 14, with her loved ones surrounding her, Jeanne died, just ten weeks after her husband. She was seventy-eight. Like Paul, her funeral mass was held at the Santa Barbara mission, though in the main church. She was then laid to rest beside her husband of nearly six decades at the Santa Barbara Cemetery. On her headstone, above the dates documenting her birth and death, read the apt description: An Angel Amongst Angels.

Her legacy on film was that of a beautiful creature, full of irrepressible sweetness and light, a gentle, caring girl-next-door that embodied the pure and hopeful ideals of post-war America and whose persona at the height of her fame, would represent these values as the perfect screen sweetheart. If she is not remembered as well as some of her more stalwart contemporaries, it can partially be blamed on the lack of appropriateness or importance placed on such mid-20th century values by modern society. Indeed, during her heyday, at exactly the time that such principles were at the forefront of thought for homeward bound G.I.s and the women who waited for them, Jeanne Crain found her greatest popularity.

In her personal life, she is remembered for her large and beautiful family, and her long, if not perfect, marriage to the same man. A rarity in Hollywood, if not an improbability. Her love of travel was a passion she had followed since her first trip on location to the middle west to film *Home in Indiana*. This yearning to see new places and meet different people took her around the globe, and yet, she would often

(Courtesy of the Jeanne Crain Brinkman Family Trust)

repeat the old proverb, "Wherever you go, there you are." For Jeanne, it meant you have to face yourself sooner or later. Having lived a fabulous life, filled with glamour and excitement, there would always be the realities of life to face on her home turf.

Although she never received a degree, she was a lifelong student, a voracious reader of philosophy, religion, art history, poetry, literature and theater. Her interests were varied and intense. She encouraged her children to be creative, to learn, to read. She passed down her love of art, and nurtured those of her offspring who found an affinity for it. When it came to the business of making films, however, she made it clear to her children that she did not recommend it as a career, and strongly advised them not to partake in it. This discouragement extended even to her grandchildren. When her oldest granddaughter, Bret, announced she wanted to pursue acting, Jeanne, who had long been out of the entertainment field, responded, "*Why*! It is such an awful business. Why would you ever want to be in it?" Most followed her counsel and went a different route, with the exception of her eldest child, Paul, Jr. After spending much of his early adulthood as an attorney, he began a career behind the camera, working with many whom he had known as a youngster in Hollywood.

Even with her star status at Twentieth Century-Fox, Crain shared many of the same traits as the characters she portrayed on the screen. The unpretentious niceness she illuminated in her movies translated behind the scenes, where she would always take the time to know the crews on her films. Punctual and polite on the movie set, and patient with the demands of stardom, Jeanne was known in the industry as being accessible and caring. Her generosity and warmth was reflected in a golden, radiant and beautiful woman.

Despite being very active socially for much of her professional life, and with a large, bustling household in her personal one, Jeanne was a very private individual who loved nothing more than sitting and reading or sketching for hours on end. She was able to enjoy all the trappings that a

Hollywood career could afford her, yet still raise a family who loved and respected her and looked to her as the central figure on whom they all could reflect. She always said she would rather have an armful of babies to a scrapbook full of screen credits, but in her case, she got both.

A Note to Loyal Readers and Classic Movie Fans

If you enjoyed what you just read (and I truly hope you did as I thoroughly enjoyed writing it), I hope you will consider leaving a positive and favorable comment/review on Amazon. A positive review is important to independent authors and only takes a moment.

Also, if you'd like to read more about classic Hollywood and the movies it produced, feel free to check out my other books and e-Magazines at my Amazon author page or check out a sampling of the titles listed below. I thank you for your interest in my work and genuinely appreciate your support.

Other Books on Classic Movies by Rupert Alistair

The Name Below the Title: 20 Classic Movie Character Actors From Hollywood's Golden Age

Hollywood and the Home Front: 25 Fabulous Films from the Forties

Sin and Vice in Black & White: 15 Classic Pre-Code Movies

The Search for Scarlett O'Hara: Gone with the Wind and Hollywood's Most Famous Casting Call

Classic Movies: 14 Films You May Not Have Seen, But Should

Classic Movie Gems: 16 MORE Films You May Not Have Seen, But Should

ACKNOWLEDGEMENTS

Besides being a classic movie lover, I am also an avid genealogist and researcher, and the past year has definitely been a journey for me, one which reached back to the beginning of the 20th-century and continued on into the beginning of this new one. It was a journey, indeed, as one discovery would lead to another and another and often two or three at a time. The research on a most favored star from Hollywood's golden age was interesting to say the least. Until I started to delve into it, I didn't realize there was so much about Jeanne Crain's life among the records, archives and repositories of this country, but I came up with a rich treasure of information that hadn't come to light before, not for the average classic movie fan, at least.

More than just my time and research was involved, however. There were others, genealogists, friends and fellow film lovers, who helped me out greatly, and to whom I'm deeply grateful. Norma Schumow and Larry Pumphrey, for helping with local California and vital record upheaval. Ross Flint and Thomas Brown for sharing their treasure trove of vintage magazine articles. Members of the Crain and Brinkman families have contributed greatly. Many thanks to Koreen Pedgenski, and Bret Crain.

Jeanne raised a large family, and to three of her offspring I am truly thankful. Jeanine Brinkman for her insight and family remembrances. Paul Brinkman, Jr., an interesting, friendly and kind gentleman, whose reminiscences and family history were fascinating. Lastly, but most definitely not least, my sincere and everlasting gratitude to Lisabette Brinkman. Our correspondence was not only informative, with stories, memories and insight into her family's life, but warm, gracious and inviting. Her enthusiasm was infectious and her efforts toward the project tireless. Her contributions included not only vital information about her mother and other family members, but a vast photographic record of their life together. My most heartfelt thanks.

NOTES AND REFERENCES

Heartland Heritage, West Coast Dreams

1. The level plains of the area's farmland: granvillenorthdakoka.com History of Egg Creek Township
2. clearing $5,000 a year: *The Pioneer Express* (Pembina, ND), April 26, 1907
3. "320 acres of corn knee high": *The Ward County Independent* (Minot, Ward County, ND), June 30, 1921
4. the local school was situated: historicmapworks.com Egg Creek Township, 1910
5. When he graduated: *Mouse River Farmers Press*, July 15, 1976
6. he became very: "SATG Glee Club Will Be Organized Here," *Grand Forks Herald*, November 18, 1918
7. and getting his poetry published: *The Poets of the Future: A College Anthology for 1920-1921*, Stratford, 1921
8. Dr. J. G. Arneberg: professional advertisement, *Turtle Mountain Star*, Rolla, ND, May 25, 1911
9. The Arneberg Prizes: The University of North Dakota, General Catalog, 1921-1922, May 1922
10. one-act play, *Kara: Plays for the Country Theatre*, Alexander Magnus Drummond, New York State College of Agriculture, Cornell University, 1922
11. The idea for the story: *Quarterly Journal - University of North Dakota*, Volume 11, 1921
12. *Kara*, along with two other: "Playmakers Ready for Production of Original Playlets." *Grand Forks Herald*, May 31, 1920, MEMORIAL DAY NOON EDITION
13. In September 1918: *The Quarterly Journal of the University of North Dakota*, Volume 11, 1920, pages 268-69
14. Crain spent much of the autumn: US Passport Application, George Crain, US Department of State, December 20, 1921
15. who was trying her hand: "White Slavery Whistleblower," *Dakota Datebook*, prairiepublic.org, January 6, 2005
16. George asked Ruth to vouch: US Passport Application, George Crain

17. In October 1922, Crain wrote: "George Crain, Exchange Student, Says He Likes So. American Country." *Grand Forks Herald.*, October 28, 1922, page 10
18. he accepted the position: The School of Education Record of the University of North Dakota, October 1923, page 5
19. Born in County Mayo, Ireland: Death Certificate for Martin Joseph Carr, State of California, filed December 15, 1947
20. After graduating from Ray High: "Ray High School Has Commencement," *Grand Forks Daily Herald*, Grand Forks, ND, June 28, 1919
21. Loretta enrolled in the teaching program: The Bulletin, State Normal School, Valley City, North Dakota, Thirteenth Annual Catalogue, May 1920
22. The couple married: Superior Court of Los Angeles County, Crain vs Crain, Complaint for Divorce, April 29, 1932
23. Loretta always wanted twins: "Jeanne Crain: Life Story." *Modern Screen*, May 1945, page 31
24. when Jeanne was told: Ibid.
25. Between 1920 and 1925, Inglewood: cityofinglewood.org/about/city_history.asp
26. a baby girl was stillborn: #9245 Standard Certificate of Birth, State of California, Filed December 12, 1928
27. almost died after developing: *Modern Screen*, May 1945, page 32
28. The Carr family had also moved: 1926 Los Angeles City Directory
29. During their childhood: *Modern Screen*, December 1946, page 31
30. According to her complaint filed in a Los Angeles divorce court: Superior Court of Los Angeles County, Crain vs Crain, Complaint for Divorce, April 29, 1932
31. The abuse continued: Ibid.
32. Loretta was, however, a good seamstress: Correspondence with Lisabette Brinkman
33. Jeanne was dreamy and withdrawn: *Modern Screen*, May 1945, page 32
34. "I was a quiet, introspective child": Hannsberry, *Femme Noir: Bad Girls of Film*
35. "Tom and Huck were more real": *Modern Screen*, May 1945, page 103
36. "always ready to wrestle": *Modern Screen*, May 1945, page 32
37. Rita would often be sick: Lisabette Brinkman

38. Enjoyed immensely: *Modern Screen*, May 1945, page 104
39. Sister Mary Miles: "Thanksgiving for Jeanne." *Modern Screen*, December 1946, page 33
40. "I came out of my shell": Hannsberry, *Femme Noir: Bad Girls of Film*
41. Since she and Rita were small: *Modern Screen*, December 1946, page 33
42. "with 2,500 students and half of them *boys*!": Ibid
43. She would remain a devout Catholic: Lisabette Brinkman
44. Dresses for the occasion: *Modern Screen*, May 1945, page 104

Orson Welles and the Beauty Queen

45. By 1939, Loretta was working full-time: 1940 US Census, Los Angeles, California
46. Jeanne and seventeen other girls: "Blonde Wins Beauty Contest." *Los Angeles Times*, July 26, 1941, page 1
47. The event was sponsored by the American Legion: "Twenty-One Compete Today for 'Miss California' Title." *Los Angeles Times*, July 25, 1941, page 3
48. There, in front of a crowd: *Los Angeles Times*, July 26, 1941, page 1
49. The blonde, hazel-eyed beauty: "Beauties Explain Urge to Be 'Miss America'." *Los Angeles Times*, July 23, 1941, page A2
50. Both Jeanne and La Planche were actually too young: www.missamerica.org/our-miss-americas/1940/1941
51. Four days after the Miss California contest: Kahn Memo, July 29, 1942, Ivan Kahn Papers, Margaret Herrick Library
52. She read a scene: "Sweet and Lovely," *Modern Screen*, February 1945, page 107
53. "Not that I fooled them much": "Fame Came the Easy Way." *Picturegoer*, March 29, 1947, page 11
54. were treated to a tour: *Modern Screen*, May 1945, page 105
55. Radio-Keith-Orpheum was born: Jewell and Harbin, *The RKO Story*, page 8
56. While visiting RKO: *Modern Screen*, February 1945, page 33
57. which would start shooting: "Screen News." *Los Angeles Times*, July 23, 1941, page 15
58. He gave her ten pages of dialogue: *Modern Screen*, February 1945, page 33

59. In a 1917 issue of *Metropolitan* magazine: Brady, *Citizen Welles: A Biography of Orson Welles*
60. On the allotted day Loretta accompanied her daughter: *Modern Screen*, February 1945, page 75
61. She was either too young: *Modern Screen*, May 1945, page 105
62. Welles interviewed more than: *Hollywood*, April 1942, page 15
63. According to Baxter's account: Bawden, Miller, *Conversations with Classic Film Stars: Interviews from Hollywood's Golden Era*, page 142
64. She appeared in the senior class play: 1942 Inglewood High School Yearbook
65. Westwood Ice Arena: "Trojan-Monarch Puck Feud Resumes Tonight." *Los Angeles Times*, January 30, 1942, page 19
66. dedication of the first ski: "Southland Snow Fans Hail Ski Chair Lift." *Los Angeles Times*, January 25, 1942, page A11
67. Sponsored by the Long Beach: "Long Beach Picks Camera Girl of '42." *Los Angeles Times*, April 13, 1942, page 8
68. Entries were submitted early: *The Daily Mail* (Hagerstown, Maryland), April 9, 1942, page 8
69. Although she was still only sixteen: *Modern Screen*, May 1945, page 107
70. Ulmanek was named runner-up: "Long Beach Picks Camera Girl of '42." *Los Angeles Times*, April 13, 1942, page 8
71. Loretta called him: Kahn Memo, April 16, 1942, Ivan Kahn Papers, Margaret Herrick Library
72. who felt Mortensen's work: Enyeart, *Willard Van Dyke: Changing the World Through Photography and Film*, page 75
73. When asked about his distaste: Teiser, Harroun, *Conversations with Ansel Adams*, page 121
74. The photographer would declare: *Modern Screen*, May 1951, page 104
75. For the duration of their shoots: Mortensen, Lytle, Coleman, Moynihan, *American Grotesque: The Life and Art of William Mortensen*, page 83-85
76. Crain would later remember: *Monsters and Madonnas: The World of William Mortensen*, Documentary Film, 1963
77. Mortensen photographed Jeanne: *The Daily Reporter* (Dover, Ohio), March 27, 1954, page 3

78. dressed as St. Bernadette: Mortensen, Lytle, Coleman, Moynihan, *American Grotesque: The Life and Art of William Mortensen*, page 83-85
79. attention of impresario Max Reinhardt: "C for Circe." *Photoplay*, December 1944, page 87
80. Reinhardt was impressed: *The Courier-Journal* (Louisville, Kentucky), July 1, 1945, Page 23
81. 20th Century-Fox purchased: *Motion Picture Herald*, July 25, 1942, page 52
82. Also in the audience: *Modern Screen*, February 1945, page 107
83. "I think this girl": Kahn Memo, October 30, 1942, Ivan Kahn Papers, Margaret Herrick Library
84. Loretta received a letter: Letter from Marie Rousseau, October 31, 1942, Jeanne Crain correspondence, Margaret Herrick Library
85. "This girl has real beauty: Kahn Memo, November 18, 1942, Ivan Kahn Papers, Margaret Herrick Library
86. Fox viewed a 16-mm color test: Ibid.
87. she received and signed a contract: *Variety*, February 10, 1943, page 4
88. The standard agreement paid: Hannsberry, *Femme Noir: Bad Girls of Film*

Zanuck and His Rising Star

89. "wiry, high-domed man": *Time*, June 12, 1950, page 64
90. In September 1942, he was granted leave: Behlmer. *Memo from Darryl F. Zanuck: The Golden Years at Twentieth Century-Fox*, page 63
91. Los Angeles superior court: *The Times* (Hammond, Indiana), April 16, 1943, page 62
92. she signed a long-term pact: *Medford Mail Tribune*, June 4, 1943, page 2
93. Jeanne was summoned to the studio: *Modern Screen*, May 1945, page 108
94. Jeanne and June were just two: "20th-Fox Grooming 5 Femmes.," *The Film Daily*, Thursday, August 26, 1943
95. began production in mid-September, 1943: *Motion Picture Daily*, September 14, 1943, page 8

96. Jeanne and Lon McCallister spent two weeks: *Modern Screen*, May 1944
97. Much of the rural landscapes: *Modern Screen*, May 1944, page 20
98. Jeanne and other cast members traveled east: *Modern Screen*, May 1944, page 20
99. "She was plastered with lipstick": Parish, *The Fox Girls*, page 564
100. the production was delayed: *Motion Picture Daily*, December 24, 1943, page 5
101. After filming was completed: Fujiwara, *The World and Its Double: The Life and Work of Otto Preminger*, page 33
102. Preminger found his young: Hirsch, *Otto Preminger: The Man Who Would Be King*
103. "In my opinion Jeanne Crain: *Motion Picture*, Volume 69, page 107
104. According to Preminger, Pallette was: Preminger, *Preminger: An Autobiography*, page 84
105. "There was much excitement: Fujiwara, *The World and Its Double: The Life and Work of Otto Preminger*, page 33
106. The Legion of Decency, always combating: *Motion Picture Daily*, September 21, 1944, page 7
107. Jeanne's name was starting to show up: *Photoplay*, December 1943, pages 14 and 120
108. she received a Christmas card from Texas: Christmas card from Opal and Raymond Garvin, December 14, 1943, Jeanne Crain correspondence, Margaret Herrick Library
109. she was given Sonja Henie's dressing room: *Daily Review* (Hayward, California), January 13, 1944, page 5
110. She was invited to the Zanuck home: "Memo to a Starlet: Jeanne Crain," *Screenland*, July 1945, page 83
111. When *Home in Indiana* was finally released: "193 Houses Set for 'Indiana' Premiere." *Motion Picture Daily*, Monday, June 12, 1944, page 3
112. who had never been outside California: *The Film Daily*, Friday, December 7, 1945, page 13; *Modern Screen*, February 1945, page 109
113. was present for a personal appearance: *Motion Picture Herald*, June 24, 1944, page 94
114. A massive war bond rally: Ibid.

115. Along with June Haver, Jeanne arrived: Ibid.
116. She met back up with Haver in Cleveland: Ibid.
117. enjoying a layover: *Showmen's Trade Review*. June 24, 1944, page 40
118. she was given a new contract: *Photoplay*, December 1944, page 87
119. She was also announced: *Motion Picture Daily*, July 5, 1944, page 9
120. *Film Daily* noted: *The Film Daily*, September 22, 1944, page 10
121. *Variety* was like-minded in its criticism: *Variety*, September 20, 1944, page 10
122. As early as May: *Motion Picture Daily*, May 23, 1944, page 3
123. It was announced in August: *The Film Daily*, August 23, 1944, page 6
124. Acclaimed stage director Lee Strasberg: *Motion Picture Herald*, August 19, 1944, page 35
125. In late October 1944, Fox: *Motion Picture Daily*, October 23, 1944, page 6
126. When Wyler was called: McGilligan, *George Cukor: A Double Life*, page 178
127. Columnist Walter Winchell had the two: "What's Happening to Lon McCallister Now!" *Screenland*, October 1944, page 74
128. McAllister made it clear though: "My G.I. Dates." *Photoplay*, January 1945, page 48
129. "You've shown remarkable progress": *Modern Screen*, February 1945, page 109
130. She enjoyed working with Cukor: *Modern Screen*, May 1945, page 108
131. Jeanne began a daily, two-hour: *Modern Screen*, February 1945, page 109
132. she began to gain a reputation: *Films in Review*, Volume 20, National Board of Review of Motion Pictures, 1969
133. The studio was promoting her: *Showmen's Trade Review*, December 16, 1944, page 10
134. She continued personal appearances: *The Tucson Liberator*, December 20, 1944
135. The studio had revived interest: *The New York Times*, October 18, 1944, page 25

136. Then, in early November: *Motion Picture Daily*, November 8, 1944, page 11

Twentieth Century-Fox Presents "The Girl Next Door"

137. predicted that before year's end: "I Predict..." *Photoplay*, January 1945, page 27
138. Despite the squeaky-clean image: Leslie, *Iowa State Fair: Country Comes to Town*, p. 92
139. traveled west from New York: *Variety*, June 16, 1943, page 2
140. The initial plan was to cast: *Motion Picture Daily*, June 16, 1943, page 2
141. The rationale was that a successful: *Variety*, August 11, 1943, page 46
142. the songwriting duo wouldn't: *Variety*, November 17, 1943, page 49
143. "We made sure, though, that our contract: Rodgers, *Musical Stages: An Autobiography*, Da Capo Press, 2009, pp. 235-236)
144. In late October, 1944: *Motion Picture Daily*, October 25, 1944, page 6
145. negotiations were taking place: *The Film Daily*, October 18, 1944, page 14
146. she was dubbed by: Mel Torme. *My Singing Teachers*, Oxford Univ. Press, 1994, page 186
147. In February, pleased with her: *Motion Picture Herald*, February 10, 1945, page 41
148. Zanuck paid $100,000: *Motion Picture Daily*, May 18, 1944, page 2
149. November, Bankhead: "Looking at Hollywood," *Chicago Tribune*, November 20, 1944, page 18
150. Zanuck had already assigned: *Waterloo Daily Courier*, September 28, 1944, page 23
151. Fox newcomer Faye Marlowe: *Hollywood Reporter*, January 18, 1945
152. Production began: *Motion Picture Herald*, May 26, 1945, page 35
153. Gene Tierney reported for work: *Modern Screen*, February 1946, page 14)
154. She reflected on her experience: Tierney, Herskowitz, *Self-Portrait*

155. He finished up: "Cornel Wilde," *Modern Screen*, July 1946, page 78
156. Rita, who was now attending: *Screenland*, October 1945, page 62
157. "almost tore the roof off": *The Film Daily*, August 14, 1945, page 3
158. Parades, street carnivals: *The Film Daily*, August 30, 1945, page 7
159. Zanuck claiming it: Behlmer, *Memo from Darryl F. Zanuck: The Golden Years at Twentieth Century-Fox*, page 92
160. When she ran into her youthful crush: *Screenland*, January 1946, page 34
161. she was number: *The Des Moines Register*, Sunday, October 14, 1945, page 45
162. this resulted in yet another: *Box Office Digest*, September 8, 1945, page 4
163. In March, while *State Fair* was shooting: *Focus on Film*, Issues 26-37. Tantivy Press, 1977
164. In the summer, it was announced: *Film Bulletin*, September 17, 1945, page 15
165. September she would be paired: *Motion Picture Herald*, September 29, 1945, page 39
166. It was one of the biggest premieres: *The Ottawa Journal*, December 21, 1945, Page 2
167. Tyrone Power, recently returned: *The Ottawa Journal*, December 21, 1945, page 2
168. The notices were kind: *The Film Daily*, December 20, 1945
169. and about Jeanne specifically: *British Journal of Photography*, Volume 93, William Crookes, T.A. Malone, George Shadbolt, 1946, page 157
170. *Leave Her to Heaven* making more: *Memo from Darryl F. Zanuck*, page 81

Paul

171. She lived with Loretta: *Modern Screen*, May 1945, page 109; California Voter Roll, 1944; 1946
172. It was a normal home: *Modern Screen*, May 1945, page 109
173. Since she was under twenty-one: *Photoplay*, April 1946, page 96

174. Theirs was a one-car household: *Screenland*, January 1946, page 89
175. Even when there was a Fox related: *Modern Screen*, April 1946, page 41
176. His father, Fred: San Francisco City Directory, 1920, sfgenealogy.co
177. an automobile dealership: *Motor World Wholesale*, Chilton Company, 1921
178. became a financier of cars: San Francisco City Directory, 1927, sfgenealogy.co
179. After graduation: *Los Angeles Times*, October 5, 2003; University of California at Berkeley Yearbook, 1937, 1938
180. Paul worked part-time: 1940 US Census
181. Mocambo with Mary Hay Barthelmess: *The Fresno Bee The Republican* (Fresno, California), October 27, 1941, Page 6
182. he was spotted: *The Fresno Bee The Republican* (Fresno, California), June 25, 1942, Page 8
183. squiring Ginger Rogers: *The Gaffney Ledger*, August 4, 1942, page 4
184. the summer of 1942: *Screenland*, August 1942, page 77
185. "an item all over again": *Pittsburgh Post-Gazette*, Mar 22, 1943, page 20
186. "the poor man's Errol Flynn": *Screenland*, August 1942, page 77
187. looked so much like Flynn: *The Cincinnati Enquirer* (Cincinnati, Ohio), April 16, 1944, Page 70
188. Brinkman met Jeanne: *Modern Screen*, April 1946, page 94
189. Jeanne and Loretta were driving: "How I Met My Husband." *Motion Picture*, Volumes 71-72, 1946, page 62-64
190. Crain later recalled: Ibid.
191. Their first official date: *Modern Screen*, April 1946, page 94
192. "I was wearing a white taffeta dress: "Runaway Bride." *Photoplay*, April 1946, page 96
193. Besides his handsome looks: "How to Keep Marriage Romantic." *Photoplay*, February 1949, page 105
194. Paul also seeing: *St. Louis Post-Dispatch*, July 31, 1944, Page 19
195. By the end of 1944: *St. Louis Post-Dispatch*, December 1, 1944, Page 41
196. For Christmas: *Photoplay*, April 1946, page 96-97

197. he joined fifty-one other: *Motion Picture Herald*, May 6, 1944, page 32
198. In an attempt to put Flynn: Goodman, *The Fifty-Year Decline and Fall of Hollywood*, page 107
199. "Hollywood is also bored: "Cal York's Gossip of Hollywood," *Photoplay*, July 1944, page 6
200. "Warner's signing of Paul Brinkman: *The Tipton Daily* (Tipton, Indiana), May 2, 1944, Page 4
201. Will McLaughlin noted: *The Ottawa Journal*, August 26, 1944, Page 9
202. It was described by exhibitors: *Motion Picture Herald*, May 5, 1945, page 45
203. His time at Warners was brief: *Photoplay*, February 1945, page 12
204. he had secured his release: *The Daily Clintonian* (Clinton, Indiana), October 13, 1944, Page 4
205. Still not exclusive with Paul: *Photoplay*, April 1946, page 97
206. Fox backed Mrs. Crain up: *The Salt Lake Tribune*, Utah, March 7, 1945, Page 16 Feeling pressure from both the studio and her mother,
207. Jeanne appeased Loretta: *Motion Picture*, Volumes 71-72, 1946, page 62-64
208. obtaining a patent: U.S. Patent Office, Des. 145, 508, Filed October 8, 1945
209. on V-J Day: *Motion Picture*, Volumes 71-72, 1946, page 62-64
210. Loretta wasn't happy: *Modern Screen*, April 1946, page 97
211. "many stormy scenes and tears": *Modern Screen*, April 1946, page 66
212. Mrs. Crain had insisted: *Motion Picture*, Volumes 71-72, 1946, page 62-64
213. When her daughter didn't return: *Photoplay*, April 1946, page 99
214. Paul took Jeanne to Marshall: *Modern Screen*, April 1946, page 97
215. Although she was "terribly worried": "Actress Due to Wed, Fails to Return Home," *San Bernardino Sun*, December 31, 1945, page 1
216. Reverend Eugene Ivancovich married: *Photoplay*, April 1946, page 30

217. Jeanne's ensemble was completely white: *Modern Screen*, April 1946, page 97
218. The witnesses were Bobby Kester: State of California, Department of Public Health, Certificate of Registry of Marriage, Paul Brinkman and Jeanne Crain, Filed January 3, 1946
219. Jeanne wanted to contact her mother: *Modern Screen*, April 1946, page 97
220. After a bridal breakfast: *Photoplay*, May 1946, page 121
221. The couple then drove away: *Motion Picture*, Volumes 71-72, 1946, page 62-64

1946 – The Year of Jeanne

222. The Brinkman's honeymoon ended: "Columbia Net Premieres New Drama Program Tomorrow." *Toledo Blade*, January 5, 1946, page 18
223. when asked by a Hollywood reporter: *Motion Picture*, 1946, Volume 71, page 8
224. As a wedding gift: *Modern Screen*, April 1946 page 97
225. Zanuck sent Ford a memo: *Memo from Darryl F. Zanuck*, page 103
226. fan mail had increased: *The Pittsburgh Press*, January 6, 1946, page 53
227. *Life* magazine recognized: *Life*, November 4, 1946, page 137
228. As early as January 1945: *The Film Daily*, January 31, 1945, page 3
229. Cornel Wilde, her costar: *Screenland*, April 1946 page 62
230. Robert Webb, wanted: *The Saturday Evening Post*, May 31, 1947, page 92
231. Webb later recalled: *The Saturday Evening Post*, May 31, 1947, page 92
232. About three hundred UN students: "The Movie Star Nevada Never Claimed." *Nevada Historical Society Quarterly*, The Society, 2001 page 261
233. Social security applications: *The University of Nevada Sagebrush*, January 18, 1946, page 6
234. The temperature was four degrees: What's Happening in Hollywood; News of Current Pictures, Trends, and Production, Motion Picture Association of America. Department of Studio and Public Service

235. Veteran character actress Hattie McDaniel: *Newcastle News*, February 21, 1946, page 12
236. "[Jeanne] spent her honeymoon: McClelland, *Forties film talk: oral histories of Hollywood*, page 193
237. when the company went: *Screenland*, August 1946, page 81
238. Paul would go skiing: *Reno Gazette-Journal*, February 13, 1946, Page 14
239. One newspaper item noted: *The Cincinnati Enquirer*, February 13, 1946, page 6
240. Defending her husband: *Screenland*, August 1946, page 81
241. Nonetheless, the "too frequent visits": *Modern Screen*, May 1946, page 64
242. The studio had been wary: "Advising Husbands Peeve Studio Heads." *Winnipeg Tribune*, March 11, 1946, page 2
243. Shortly after these stories: *Kingsport News*, March 18, 1946, page 4
244. The trip to Reno: *Photoplay*, May 1946, page 124
245. During the filming: Jeanne Crain Correspondence, February 4, 1946, Margaret Herrick Library
246. she and director King: "Director and Star are Honor Guests at Dinner Party." *Nevada State Journal*, February 3, 1946, Page 7
247. Crain would later remember: *Nevada State Journal*, May 25, 1975, page 10
248. Accompanied by her new husband: *The Film Daily*, July 9, 1946, page 2
249. The three-day event: *The Film Daily*, July 11, 1946, page 7
250. Bosley Crowther: *New York Times*, July 18, 1946
251. Fox renewed Crain's: Showmen's Trade Review, August 17, 1946, page 37
252. With *Margie*, the Roxy: *Motion Picture Daily*, October 24, 1946, page 8
253. it set pre-release box-office: *Motion Picture Daily*, November 14, 1946, page 1
254. The film made its western: *The University of Nevada Sagebrush*, November 1, 1946, page 3
255. She was expecting a baby: (*Independent Exhibitors Film Bulletin*, November 25, 1946, page 18)

Motherhood and Addie Ross

256. She denied that she was expecting: *Modern Screen*, January 1947, page 106
257. Upon the suggestion of Huntington Hartford: *Modern Screen*, April 1946 page 97
258. They acquired the land: *Modern Screen*, November 1946, page 70
259. By spring 1946: *Honolulu Star-Bulletin*, April 17, 1946, page 8
260. A lavish affair: *Modern Screen*, September 1947, page 117
261. After Shah-Shah escaped: *The Wilkes-Barre Record*, October 31, page 10
262. Jeanne began taking: *Middletown Times Herald* (Middletown, New York), November 23, 1946, page 2; *Brooklyn Eagle*, January 20, 1947, page 6
263. In early February: *Motion Picture Daily*, February 5, 1947, page 12
264. she was announced to star: *The Film Daily*, February 14, 1947, page 8
265. Early expectations had her: *The Odessa American*, February 3, 1947, page 3
266. On the Saturday before Easter: *Modern Screen*, July 1947, page 116
267. The plate-glassed walls: "Jeanne Moves to New Home." *Harrisburg Telegraph*, August 22, 1947, page 11
268. an addition afforded: "How to Keep Marriage Romantic." *Photoplay*, February 1949, page 105
269. Complaints began coming in: *Los Angeles Times*, August 26, 1947, page 11
270. Jeanne and Paul reluctantly: *Annapolis Capital* Newspaper Archives, August 27, 1947
271. The week after the lioness: *The Cumberland News*, September 1, 1947, page 6
272. Jeanne canceled the trip: *The Daily Clintonian*, September 29, 1947, page 4
273. After *The Flaming Age: Asbury Park Press*, October 24, 1947, page 7
274. Charles Feldman, a leading Hollywood: *The Indianapolis Star*, September 10, 1947, page 20
275. Although one movie trade: *Independent Exhibitor's Film Bulletin*, October 11, 1948, page 18

276. Also, Orson Welles: *Harrisburg Telegraph*, September 15, 1947, page 15
277. Of Jeanne's performance: *Showmen's Trade Review*, January 24, 1948, page 19
278. Another film being produced: *Arizona Republic*, October 14, 1947, page 9
279. Before he signed: Chierichetti, *George Seaton*, page 117-118
280. Director Seaton revealed: Ibid
281. Bosley Crowther: *New York Times*, October 16, 1948
282. *Variety* also sang her praises: *Variety*, September 15, 1948, page 15
283. Upon its general release: *Variety*, January 5, 1949, page 46
284. Jeanne's career got another: *Variety*, April 21, 1948, page 17
285. Crain and Baxter were also slated: Staggs, *All About All About Eve: The Complete Behind-the-Scenes Story of the Bitchiest Film Ever Made*, page 172)
286. The novelization was featured: Behlmer, page 153)
287. Baxter was out: Geist, *Pictures Will Talk: The Life and Films of Joseph L. Mankiewicz*, page 138
288. Mankiewicz traveled to the East: *The Film Daily*, May 28, 1948, page 2
289. Jeanne and her fellow "wives": *Pittsburgh Post-Gazette*, June 28, 1948, page 28
290. Linda even accompanied Jeanne: *Madera Tribune*, June 23, 1948, page 2
291. He would later vent: Dauth, Joseph L. Mankiewicz: Interviews, page 191
292. In 1946, he had requested: Joseph L. Mankiewicz Papers, 28-f.328, memo to Darryl F. Zanuck, dated May 31, 1946, Margaret Herrick Library
293. The sultry star had to be replaced: *Screenland*, November 1948, page 66
294. One reporter put it less delicately: "Make Way for Youth," *Modern Screen*, May 1949, page 100
295. She wanted to work: *Modern Screen*, July 1949, page 83
296. Preminger was able to start: *Showmen's Trade Review*, July 17, 1948, page 29
297. Her condition only showed: *Modern Screen*, July 1949, page 83
298. Bosley Crowther: *New York Times*, April 2, 1949

299. *Variety*, however, took a completely: *Variety*, April 6, 1949, page 8
300. The expectant mother: "How to Keep Marriage Romantic." *Photoplay*, February 1949, page 43
301. January 21, 1949: *San Bernardino Sun*, January 23, 1949, page 22

Pinky

302. "as autonomous as any": Pratley, *The Cinema of Otto Preminger*, page 68
303. It was selected: *Current Biography 1954*: Cid Ricketts Sumner
304. Preminger asked him: Pratley, page 68
305. Zanuck simply shrugged: Mosley, *Zanuck: The Rise and Fall of Hollywood's Last Tycoon*, page 238
306. "These things are inevitable": Pratley, page 68
307. Zanuck took on: *Showmen's Trade Review*, January 29, 1949, page 28
308. Ford was seen: McBride. *Searching for John Ford: A Life*, page 488
309. Zanuck, however, was very clear: Behlmer, page 162
310. Lena Horne: Gavin, *Stormy Weather: The Life of Lena Horne*, page 208
311. A week before Michael's: *Dramatics*, Vol. 20-21, International Thespian Society, 1948, page 19
312. In February, she was tentatively: *Variety*, February 23, 1949, page 6
313. According to one motion picture: Bogle, *Toms, Coons, Mulattoes, Mammies, & Bucks: An Interpretive History of Blacks in American Films*, page 152
314. There was also conflict: Waters, Samuels, *His Eye is On the Sparrow: An Autobiography*, page 272
315. Zanuck later recalled: Gussow, *Darryl F. Zanuck: Don't Say Yes Until I Finish Talking*, page 151
316. He tried directing: *Showmen's Trade Review*, March 26, 1949, page 37-38
317. He then developed: *Motion Picture Daily*, April 1, 1949, page 3
318. It was estimated: *Variety*, April 6, 1949, page 18
319. According to Kazan: Kazan, *Elia Kazan: A Life*, page 374
320. "Jack's not sick": Ibid.

321. According to Kazan: Ibid.
322. "She was a good soul: Ibid.
323. He would later call Crain: "Rex Reed Reports." *Chicago Tribune*, February 6, 1972, page 9
324. During filming: *Dramatics*, International Thespian Society, 1948, page 19
325. *Variety* made the observation: *Variety*, March 2, 1948
326. "excellent casting: *Movie Makers*, 1949, page 422
327. Joseph Breen, eventually: Motion Picture Association of America. Production Code Administration records, Production files. Margaret Herrick Library
328. The production also got input: "Pinky: Story on Girl Who Passes Will Be Most Debated Film of Year." *Ebony*, September 1949, page 23
329. She confided: Ibid.
330. Upon its Atlanta: *Showmen's Trade Review*, November 26, 1949, page 9
331. Marshall, Texas: Lev, *Twentieth Century-Fox: The Zanuck-Skouras Years, 1935–1965*, page 148
332. One reviewer proclaimed: *Harrison's Reports*, October 1, 1949, page 159
333. while another went: *Focus: A Film Review*, January 1950, page 14
334. "After all, it's time I grew": "Why Jeanne is Happier at 24." *Screenland*, October 1949, page 24

Teen Angst at 25

335. *Variety* named Jeanne: *Variety*, January 4, 1950, page 59
336. Zanuck signed her: *Current Biography, 1951*: Jeanne Crain, page 144
337. Granted, she was slated: *Showmen's Trade Review*, October 15, 1949
338. "After having the best": Kotsilibas-Davis, Loy, *Myrna Loy: Being and Becoming*, page 242
339. According to Crain: Ibid.
340. A short story had come: Behlmer, page 165
341. After reading: Carey, Mankiewicz, *More About All About Eve*, page 69
342. Mankiewicz was "deeply disappointed": Dauth, page 191

343. His argument against the casting: Memo from JLM to DZ, January 18, 1950, Joseph L. Mankiewicz Papers, Margaret Herrick Library
344. Sheila Graham: *Pittsburgh Post-Gazette*, February 19, 1950, page 11
345. Mankiewicz warned: Carey, Mankiewicz, page 69
346. according to Anne Baxter's account: Bawden, Miller, *Conversations with Classic Film Stars: Interviews from Hollywood's Golden*
347. scheduled to go: *Modern Screen*, October 1950, page 99
348. Crain worked out: *Screenland*, January 1951, page 10
349. whose program of diet: *Life*, July 15, 1940, page 55
350. "about time for": *San Bernardino Daily Sun*, November 25, 1950, page 3
351. Zanuck had vowed: *Film Bulletin*, January 16, 1950, page 17
352. When it was released: *Motion Picture Daily*, July 19, 1951, page 2
353. Bosley Crowther: *New York Times*, July 19, 1951
354. she "was the only actress": *San Bernardino Daily Sun*, August 7, 1951, page 4
355. the leads were cast: "Cary Grant and Anne Baxter Get Leads in Doctor's Diary." *Los Angeles Examiner*, February 23, 1951, page 7 He conceded, explaining: Carey, Mankiewicz, page 69
356. "I don't like the name Deborah: and I don't like Jeanne Crain." Geist, page 209
357. Mankiewicz did change: *Modern Screen*, June 1951, page 11
358. She had always worn: *San Bernardino Daily Sun*, April 19, 1951, page 31
359. Jeanne sent a large bottle: *Modern Screen*, April 1952, page 95
360. Jeanne received decent reviews: *Variety*, August 22, 1951
361. it was a minor film: Phillips, *George Cukor*, page 57
362. Jeanne was allowed: *Screenland*, September 1951, page 18
363. Cukor sent a letter: Cukor Letter to Zanuck, July 11, 1951, George Cukor Papers, Margaret Herrick Library
364. "If you got along well: Kotsilibas-Davis, Loy, page 259
365. The AP wire wasted: *San Bernardino Daily Sun*, November 7, 1951, page 4

Goodbye, Fox

366. ABC Die and Engineering: *USC Daily Trojan*, Vol. 43, No. 78, February 19, 1952, page 1; *Aviation Week and Space Technology*, 1952, Volume 57, page 44
367. Jeanne served: *Modern Screen*, January 1953, page 81
368. one review found: *Sight and Sound*, 1952, British Film Institute, page 77
369. It wasn't *The Robe*: *Jacksonville Daily Journal*, October 29, 1952, page 2
370. "I even get to slap: *Des Moines Register*, February 12, 1953, page 15
371. which was developed: *Saturday Review*, Saturday Review Associates, 1953, page 29
372. "beautiful but not entirely": *New York Times*, September 30, 1953
373. She and Crain became: Garrison, *Howard Hughes in Las Vegas*, page 269
374. (In turn, Hughes would: Lisabette Brinkman; Interview with Paul Brinkman, Jr.
375. one biographer noted: Gans, *Carole Landis: A Most Beautiful Girl*, page 86
376. *Vicki* was tagged: *New York Times*, September 8, 1953
377. In March, it was announced: *Hollywood Reporter*, March 1953
378. Paul built Jeanne: *The Guardian*, US Edition, Crain Obituary, December 15, 2003
379. She even claimed: *Screenland Plus TV-Land*, August 1954, page 71
380. She hadn't forgotten: *Asbury Park Press*, May 8, 1953, page 16
381. She acknowledged: "Hollywood," *Portsmouth Herald*, May 15, 1953, page 9
382. Had her final option: *Modern Screen*, August 1953, page 89
383. and she ultimately paid: Lev, page 165
384. Paul reportedly netting: *Modern Screen*, January 1954, page 65
385. Jeanne made an: *Screenland Plus TV-Land*, February 1955, page 70
386. After consulting: *Modern Screen*, August 1953, page 80
387. Bob Cat Bob: *Screenland Plus TV-Land*, February 1955, page 70
388. She then "tossed away": *Pasadena Independent*, December 14, 1955, page 52
389. Her transformation: *Modern Screen*, August 1953, page 14

390. There were also some: *Modern Screen*, December 1953, page 14
391. She became such a staple: *Modern Screen*, January 1953, page 12
392. and months later noted: *Modern Screen*, May 1953, page 88)
393. "I'm past 25": "Take My Word For It," Jeanne Crain, star columnist, *Modern Screen*, May 1953, page 77
394. Hollywood's Number One Party Girl: *Long Beach Independent*, March 18, 1955, page 27
395. was based on a story: *Film Bulletin*, May 18, 1953, page 17
396. The film was to be shot: Ibid.
397. It was a financial boon for Crain: *Modern Screen*, August 1953, page 89
398. Debbie Reynolds was slated: "Louella Parsons' Good News." *Modern Screen*, September 1953, page 12
399. the couple sailed for Europe: *Motion Picture Daily*, August 12, 1953, page 2
400. Filming in Africa: "Jeanne Crain's African Adventure," *Chicago Tribune*, February 28, 1954, page 24
401. Tragedy struck while filming: Ibid.
402. Jeanne and Paul made a three-day: Lisabette Brinkman
403. Later the same month: *San Bernardino Daily Sun*, October 28 1953, page 4
404. "I was too excited to answer": *Lubbock Morning Avalanche*, October 27, 1953, page 44
405. Jeanne agreed to: *New York Times*, February 15, 1954, page 20
406. Jeanne signed her contract: *Los Angeles Times*, April 21, 1958, page 39
407. She would be free: *Waco Tribune-Herald*, May 8, 1955, page 70
408. A decade later: *The Daily Reporter*, March 27, 1954, page 3
409. "as feeble and contrived: *New York Times*, August 9, 1954
410. Another industry scribe: *Harrison's Reports*, August 7, 1954, page 126
411. Russ-Field Corp.: Russell. *Jane Russell: An Autobiography, My Path & My Detour*, page 152
412. Crain fell in love with: "Jeanne Crain: Wife, Mother, Star." *Chicago Tribune*, August 7, 1955, page 17
413. Paul made three trips: "The Miracle of Jeanne Crain," *Modern Screen*, February 1956, page 71

414. After the holiday: *Motion Picture Daily*, January 17, 1955, page 2
415. Loretta, who saw Nader: *The Phi Gamma Delta*, Volume 79, Issue 5, 1957, page 404
416. "hiding her light under": *Los Angeles Times*, November 8, 1955, page 73
417. (the trip also allowed Paul: *Modern Screen*, February 1956, page 71
418. "one of the finest actors: *Indianapolis Star*, February 20, 1956, page 11
419. Brinkmans purchased: *Brazosport Facts*, January 25, 1956, page 8
420. Paul had just sold: *Evening Independent*, February 25, 1956, page 4
421. At the end of February: Ibid.
422. Jeanne spent a month: *Chicago Tribune*, August 7, 1955, page 17

Divorce

423. by 1955, had reached: "The Rise of the Expose Magazines." Kansas City Times, August 10, 1955, page 30
424. "one of those duck-around daddies": *Confidential*, May 1956, page 11
425. The article claimed: *Confidential*, May 1956, page 46-47
426. She retained high profile: *Edinburg Daily Courier*, March 30, 1956, page 1
427. The suit also charged: *Idaho State Journal*, March 30, 1956, page 15
428. Crain asked for custody: *Daily Independent*, March 30, 1956, page 10
429. Jeanne claimed: *Modern Screen*, July 1956, page 14
430. The alterations to their: *Greensburg Daily News*, March 16, 1957, page 10
431. "We're tearing apart our: *Indianapolis Star*, March 26, 1956, page 11
432. Jeanne still intended: *Evening Independent*, April 16, 1956, page 4
433. A week after the filing: *Evening Independent*, April 16, 1956, page 4; (karsh.org/sittings/crain)

434. Paul saw the children: *Daily Reporter*, April 21, 1956, page 4
435. Friends reported: *The Record-Argus*, May 10, 1956, page 4
436. On May 8, Paul filed: *Daily Independent Journal*, May 9, 1956, page 25
437. One complaint included Loretta: Details of Crain's amended complaint are drawn from the following: *Lubbock Evening Journal*, May 17, 1956, page 29; *The Daily Reporter* (Dover, Ohio), May 17, 1956, page 1
438. Paul responded that he: *Mason City Globe-Gazette*, May 17, 1956, page 2
439. On Friday, May 18, Jeanne appeared: *The Times* (San Mateo, California), May 19, 1956, page 16
440. Because of their children: *San Bernardino County Sun*, May 19, 1956, page 1
441. Paul threatened cross-complaint: *Evening Independent* (Massillon, Ohio), May 29, 1956, page 4
442. asked the Superior Court: *Lubbock Avalanche-Journal*, June 3, 1956, page 69
443. Paul said "I'll tell my side": *Winona Daily News*, June 8, 1956, page 4
444. Crain's friend, Bobbie Kester: *Los Angeles Times*, June 8, 1956, page 29
445. According to Crain: *Sandusky Register*, June 8, 1956, page 2
446. A hearing was set: *Monroe News-Star*, June 8, 1956, page 16
447. Powsner predicted "a real juicy hassle": *Cumberland News*, June 9, 1956, page 1
448. Brinkman then hired Arthur Crowley: "Hollywood's Forgotten Superlawyer," *The Hollywood Reporter*, March 11, 2011)
449. "Any charges of adultery": *San Bernardino Daily Sun*, June 15 1956, page 1
450. "Mrs. Brinkman has a spotless reputation": *Freeport Journal-Standard*, June 15, 1956, page 1
451. "There is absolutely no truth to the charges": Ibid.
452. Brinkman's three-page cross-complaint: "Jeanne Crain Accused of Infidelity by Her Husband." *Los Angeles Times*, June 15, 1956, page 25
453. One observer noted: *The Times* (San Mateo), June 18, 1956, page 20

454. Crain's friends backed her: *Lubbock Morning Avalanche*, June 18, 1956, page 2
455. Attorney Crowley planned: Gladstone, *The Man Who Seduced Hollywood: The Life and Loves of Greg Bautzer, Tinseltown's Most Powerful Lawyer*, page 205
456. Bautzer told the press: Gladstone, page 206
457. On June 25, the motions: *San Bernardino County Sun*, June 26, 1956, page 4
458. Crain's 66-page deposition: *Newport Daily News*, June 29, 1956, page 9
459. Rhoads was dressed: *Longview News-Journal*, June 29, 1956, page 6
460. Jeanne refused to answer: Gladstone, page 206
461. She also did not answer: *Bernardino County Sun*, June 29, 1956, page 5
462. A court session was scheduled: Gladstone, page 206
463. The day the settlement was announced: *Index-Journal*, July 12, 1956, page 15
464. Jeanne's publicity agent: *The Robesonian* (Lumberton, North Carolina), July 24, 1956, page 2
465. The couple signed: *The Times* (San Mateo), July 25, 1956, page 19
466. Jeanne would soon begin: *Anderson Daily Bulletin*, July 25, 1956, page 7
467. "I want to get involved": *The Times* (San Mateo), August 7, 1956, page 14
468. "solemnly but tearlessly" divorced Paul: (*The Times* (San Mateo, California), August 7, 1956, page 14)
469. Within ten days of the hearing: *Lebanon Daily News*, August 16, 1956, page 35
470. described as looking: *Los Angeles Times*, November 18, 1956, page 89
471. Scala "made a quick switcheroo": *Terre Haute Tribune*, August 28, 1956, page 4
472. Louella Parsons observed: *Anderson Daily Bulletin*, September 1, 1956, page 3
473. A "tall, dark, curvy Amazon,": *Modern Screen*, June 1953, page 98

474. Paul saw her regularly: *Brazil Daily Times* (Brazil, Indiana), October 8, 1956, page 5), (Dorothy Kilgallen's *Voice of Broadway, Shamolin News-Dispatch*, October 9, 1956, page 4), (*The Daily Reporter* (Dover, Ohio), November 28, 1956, page 2), (*Valley News* (Van Nuys, California), December 13, 1956, page 88)

475. "I don't see how they": *Raleigh Register*, September 5, 1956, page 4

476. she was admitted: "Actress Suffers Nervous Exhaustion." *Corsicana Daily Sun*, October 16, 1956, page 4

477. Paul asked Jeanne: *Corsicana Daily Sun*, December 15, 1956, page 8

478. a pickup order was issued: *Amarillo Globe-Times*, December 26, 1956, page 1

479. Ryan told the police: *Albany Democrat-Herald*, December 26, 1956, page 10

480. "I'm in love with her: *Evening Review*, December 26, 1956, page 3

481. Brinkman said he went: *Daily Times* (New Philadelphia, Ohio), December 27, 1956, page 9

482. Rhoads countered *Waco News-Tribune*, December 27, 1956, page 11

483. Crain said she had: *Corpus Christi Caller-Times*, December 28, 1956, page 23

484. Feldman party was a lavish: *Ogden Standard Examiner*, January 1, 1957, page 1

485. A seven-course dinner: *Medford Mail Tribune*, January 1, 1957, page 7

486. Jeanne and Paul arrived: *Berkshire Eagle*, January 1, 1957, page 1

487. "I hadn't intended": *Democrat and Chronicle*, January 2, 1957, page 13

A New Beginning

488. The belated trip: *Evening Review*, January 2, 1957, page 22

489. "maybe we'll continue": *San Bernardino County Sun*, January 13, 1957, page 50

490. "He's an old friend": *Berkshire Eagle*, January 15, 1957, page 8

491. "Jeanne and Paul really: *Daily Reporter*, January 12, 1957, page 9
492. The couple returned home: *Kokomo Tribune*, January 24, 1957, page 11
493. Paul was back in court: *Burlington Daily Times*, February 16, 1957, page 12
494. Brinkman was cleared: *Albany Democrat-Herald*, February 17, 1957, page 12
495. "Jeanne Crain is decorative": *New York Times*, March 15, 1957
496. Brinkman sold: "Electronic Industries News Briefs." *Tele-Tech & Electronics Industries*, April 1956, page 35
497. Later in the year he purchased: "Lumber Shipment Due Every 10 Days." *Press-Courier* (Oxnard, California), February 27, 1957, page 13
498. One of the assets acquired: "Behind the Scenes in Hollywood." *Index-Journal*, February 7, 1957, page 5
499. "second honeymoon" cruise: Details of the Pavane incident are drawn from the following: (*Independent* (Long Beach, California), June 26, 1957, page A-2) ("Actress, Mate Saved from Disabled Yacht." *Daily Independent Journal* (San Rafael, California), June 26, 1957, page 4) ("Yacht Voyage Almost Tragic." *San Bernardino County Sun*, June 26, 1957, page 6)
500. As a wholesale: *Press-Courier* (Oxnard, California), March 6, 1957, page 1
501. it had steadily increased: *Press-Courier*, May 6, 1957, page 9
502. Thompson charged Brinkman: *Press-Courier*, August 27, 1957, page 1; August 31, 1957, page 1
503. Brinkman settled out of court: *Pasadena Independent*, August 21, 1957, page 27
504. The week after: *Cedar Rapids Gazette*, September 5, 1957, page 2
505. Jeanne had to withdraw: *Desert Sun*, June 11, 1957, page 4
506. The doctor let Jeanne: *Pocono Record*, December 9, 1957, page 16
507. Jeanne had signed: "Louella's Movie-Go-Round" Column, *Albuquerque Journal*, December 23, 1957, page 12
508. Paul, who was set: *The Pocono Record*, January 25, 1958, page 14

509. Brinkman's legal woes: *Independent* (Long Beach), March 20, 1958, page 20
510. pleaded innocent: "Brinkman Denies Officer's Charges." *Los Angeles Times*, April 3, 1958, page 6
511. In June, a municipal judge: "Husband of Actress Wins." *Redlands Daily Facts*, June 19, 1958, page 2
512. Universal Pictures Company: *Independent*, March 20, 1958, page 6
513. Crain demanded: "$30,288 in Back Pay Asked by Jeanne Crain." *Los Angeles Times*, April 21, 1958, page 39
514. "[The children] make: *The Lincoln Star*, April 26, 1959, page 18
515. "The whole thing got to me": "Jeanne Crain Likes TV." *Shamokin News-Dispatch*, April 23, 1959, page 8
516. "Since I'd never known": *San Antonio Express*, October 12, 1958, page 79
517. the troupe rehearsed Kotsilibas-Davis, Loy, page 275
518. *Billboard's* observation: *Billboard*, May 4, 1959, page 14
519. "This is the kind of life: *Shamokin News-Dispatch*, April 23, 1959, page 8
520. When released: *Film Bulletin*, February 15, 1960, page 28
521. "No matter how long: Hannsberry, Femme Noir
522. Jeanne and Paul were considered: "Society in Hollywood." *Modern Screen*, November 1959, page 8
523. were often members: *The Morning Herald*, February 26, 1959, page 4
524. her parents were registered: California Voter Registration, Los Angeles County; 1928, 1930, 1936, 1938)
525. reverted back to her Republican: CVR, LA Co.; 1944, 1946, 1948
526. registered Republicans: (CVR, LA Co.; 1950, 1952, 1954
527. part of the Entertainment: *The Times* (San Mateo), October 6, 1952, page 13
528. she headed: *Press Democrat* (Santa Rosa), October 28, 1952, page 1
529. Jeanne was part: *Corpus Christie Caller-Times*, October 31, 1960, page 27
530. Nixon made a bid: Richard Nixon Presidential Library, White House Special Files Collection Folder List
531. When asked if she ever: *Charleston Daily-Mail*, November 3, 1960, page 2

532. A reluctant witness: "Love Affair Charges Denied by Jeanne Crain." *Los Angeles Times*, November 3, 1960, page 16
533. it took a jury: "Jury Awards $5,000 in Brinkman Suit." *Los Angeles Times*, November 4, 1960, page 12
534. Homer and Hilda Rhoads: *Kansas City Times*, May 3, 1961, page 1
535. She closed a deal: *Cumberland News*, October 6, 1960, page 18
536. Jeanne signed with Italian: *Anderson Daily Bulletin*, December 6, 1960, page 11
537. "It's an excellent role": *Greeley Daily Tribune*, November 28, 1960, page 9
538. Tentatively titled *Love & Kisses*: "Hollywood Roundup." *Weekly Television Digest*, January 9, 1961, page 11
539. *Love & Kisses* became *The Jeanne Crain Show*: "The Cowboys Are Being Put Out to Pasture." *Broadcasting Telecasting*, February 20, 1961, page 130
540. "never had a chance": TV in Review." *The Republic*, September 5, 1962, page 14
541. Jeanne signed: *The Odessa American*, January 30, 1961, page 15
542. The film, described as: *Current Biography, 1967*: David Janssen, page 197
543. While there, the three lived: Correspondence with Jeanine Brinkman
544. "I like to keep working": *Daily Times* (New Philadelphia, Ohio), July 21, 1961, page 6
545. she attended the Berlin: *Salt Lake Tribune*, July 19, 1961, page 9
546. Crain returned to Italy: *Albuquerque Journal*, September 2, 1961, page 9
547. Price took Crain: Price, *Vincent Price: A Daughter's Biography*
548. Jeanne came home: *Chicago Daily Tribune*, February 26, 1962, page 1

The Family Brinkman (and Crain)

549. "This woman did a tremendous: *The Hartford Courant*, March 3, 1962, page 17
550. Loretta could see: Paul Brinkman, Jr.

551. she garnered ohhs and ahhs: *Chicago Tribune*, August 28, 1963, page 20
552. the last two weeks: *Chicago Tribune*, September 18, 1963, page 18
553. *Please Don't Eat the Daisies: Chicago Tribune*, August 21, 1963, page 22
554. back at the Drury: *Hartford Courant*, June 20, 1964, page 20
555. Jeanne told Hedda Hopper: *Detroit Free Press*, December 23, 1964, page 11
556. "People say 'Are you playing: "Brer Rabbit and Actress Link Hands In Taffy Pull." *New York Times*, December 17, 1968, page 53
557. "They've been with us: *Santa Cruz Sentinel*, May 6, 1966, page 19
558. "I love both my children: McKay, *Dana Andrews: The Face of Noir*, page 194
559. "would never allow: Lisabette Brinkman
560. Jeanne spent most of her time: Ibid.
561. big, chaotic household: Ibid.
562. Jeanne described it: "Mama Has 7 Kids and a Yen to Work." Bob Thomas' Hollywood. *Akron Beacon Journal*, May 6, 1966, page 23
563. Jeanne was dropped: "Howard Duff Scores Again." *Philadelphia Enquirer*, August 18, 1968, page 290
564. "Given the year of its making": Kehr, "Cult Camp Classics." *New York Times*, June 26, 2007
565. "Both Andrews and Miss Crain": "'Hot Rods' Rolls Into Dead End." *Boston Globe*, May 25, 1967, page 26
566. "Frankly, I wouldn't go": "Brer Rabbit and Actress Link Hands in Taffy Pull." *New York Times*, December 17, 1968, page 53
567. "a wholesome, middle-aged": Ibid.
568. she began studying: Lisabette Brinkman
569. Brinkmans bought a home: *Los Angeles Times*, June 16, 1964, page 11
570. Jeanne became a member: "Artists for Workshops Announced." *Los Angeles Times*, June 17, 1971, page 15
571. She had a painting studio: Lisabette Brinkman
572. Crain joined a group: "Art Group Will Show Paintings by Members." *Los Angeles Times*, January 25, 1968, page 2

573. "Mortgage the house": "Jeanne Crain, Beauty at Ease with Brains." *St. Louis Post-Dispatch,* October 26, 1969, page 112
574. she and Paul seriously contemplated: Lisabette Brinkman
575. While studying at Schifrin's studio: Ibid.
576. She graced TV: "Jeanne's Still That 'Girl Next Door'." *Chicago Tribune,* May 22, 1970, page 17
577. Beverly Hills sewing circle: Lisabette Brinkman
578. Jeanne signed on: *Los Angeles Times,* July 24, 1971, page 7
579. One review summed up: *Pittsburg Press,* November 1, 1974, page 22
580. was announced: "Movie Call Sheet." *Los Angeles Times,* January 1, 1972, page 9
581. Jeanne drove herself: "Wants Back In." *Atlanta Constitution,* February 20, 1972, page 17
582. "Someone decided it was time: "No Suspense Supplied in 'Skyjacked'." Hartford Courant, June 1, 1972, page 82
583. Jeanne was urged: "Voice of Broadway." *The Monroe News-Star,* October 21, 1974, page 7
584. In front of hundreds of attorneys: "Playboy, Cutie Star in Mock Rape Trial." *Long Beach Independent,* September 13, 1974, page 12
585. The skit was in response: Ibid
586. bought land in the Sacramento River Valley: Lisabette Brinkman
587. In December 1972: "Last Minute Rush to File Ag Preserves in 1972." *Lompoc Record,* December 1, 1972, page 9
588. The whole family would enjoy: Lisabette Brinkman
589. For years she took an annual retreat: Paul Brinkman, Jr.

An Armful of Babies or a Scrapbook Full of Screen Credits

590. Bob Rousseau, died: "Dr. Rousseau Dies While on Ski Trip." *Santa Cruz Sentinel,* February 3, 1977, page 22
591. His mother, Marie, one of Loretta's sisters, passed away just five months later. (Carr Family Descendancy, courtesy of Lisabette Brinkman)
592. Her body was found: *Los Angeles Times,* September 9, 1977, page 2
593. While still in college: "Scenic Wonder." *Photoplay,* February 1946, page 61

594. had "film ambitions of her own": Graham, Sheila. "C for Circe." *Photoplay*, December 1944, page 86
595. she tried unsuccessfully *News-Press* (Fort Myers, Florida), May 3, 1949, page 4
596. sat for William Mortensen: Lisabette Brinkman
597. When he was born: Paul Brinkman, Jr.
598. Though she had suffered health problems: Lisabette Brinkman
599. When Rita married: *Los Angeles Times*, October 1, 1957, page A3; February 13, 1958, page A2
600. approached his mother about George: Paul Brinkman, Jr.
601. Jeanine, answered a knock on the door: Lisabette Brinkman, Jeanine Brinkman
602. He received a cool reception: Lisabette Brinkman
603. George and Rita became closer: Paul Brinkman, Jr.
604. When his daughter died: Lisabette Brinkman
605. helped him move into a nursing home: Paul Brinkman, Jr.
606. Besides buying Loretta the house: Lisabette Brinkman
607. Loretta suffered from hypertension: Loretta Carr Crain, Certificate of Death #22176, State of California
608. She and her son-in-law: Lisabette Brinkman
609. Free of the emotional and physical demands: Ibid.
610. Jeanne was an encouraging: Ibid.
611. "Autonomy in a relationship is crucial": Ibid.
612. By the spring of 1980: Ibid.
613. Jeanne agreed to be: *San Bernardino County Sun*, April 11, 1983, page 8
614. Paul began to spend the majority: Lisabette Brinkman
615. Paul, rarely vulnerable to his feelings: Ibid.
616. Then, in 1995, when she turned seventy: Ibid.
617. became the first guitarist for the group: *Spin*, August 2003, page 73
618. She became very sedentary and a caregiver: Lisabette Brinkman
619. She would talk on the phone: Correspondence with Koreen Pedginski
620. alcohol was no longer a problem: Lisabette Brinkman, Paul Brinkman, Jr.
621. Paul, Jr., who by this time: Paul Brinkman, Jr.
622. The Brinkman children who lived nearby: Lisabette Brinkman
623. Jeanne suffered a heart attack: Ibid.

624. "Wherever you go": Ibid.
625. When her oldest granddaughter: Correspondence with Bret Crain
626. Jeanne was a very private: Lisabette Brinkman

BIBLIOGRAPHY

Much of the information gleaned for this book was sourced from dozens of newspaper articles from across the country, many which carried syndicated columns from Hollywood and the entertainment world. Others were stories connected with Crain and her family. Another major source of information was movie fan magazines from the 1940s and 1950s, when Crain was a major star. Individual issues and page numbers are included in the Notes section, but, along with mainstream news magazines, the list of publications includes: Modern Screen, Picturegoer, Hollywood, Photoplay, Motion Picture Herald, Variety, Time, Film Daily, Screenland, Showmen's Trade Review, Films in Review, Hollywood Reporter, Box Office Digest, Focus on Film, Film Bulletin, Motion Picture, Saturday Evening Post, Ebony, Sight and Sound.

Archival Collections

Margaret Herrick Library, Academy of Motion Picture Arts and Sciences
Ivan Kahn Papers
Jeanne Crain Papers
Joseph L. Mankiewicz Papers
Production Code Administration Records
George Cukor Papers

Government and Educational Archival Collections and Reports

The Bulletin, State Normal School, Valley City, North Dakota, Thirteenth Annual Catalogue, May 1920

California Voter Registration, Los Angeles County; 1928, 1930, 1936, 1938, 1944, 1946, 1948, 1950, 1952, 1954

City Directory, Los Angeles, California, 1926

City Directory, San Francisco, California, 1920, 1927

Inglewood High School Yearbook, Inglewood, California, 1942

Nevada Historical Society Quarterly, The Society, 2001

Richard Nixon Presidential Library, White House Special Files Collection Folder List

The School of Education Record of the University of North Dakota, October 1923

Superior Court of Los Angeles County, Crain vs Crain, Complaint for Divorce, April 29, 1932

United States Federal Census, Los Angeles, California, 1940

United States Patent Office, Des. 145, 508, Filed October 8, 1945

The University of North Dakota, General Catalog, 1921-1922, May 1922

The University of North Dakota, Quarterly Journal - Volume 11, 1920, 1921

Websites

cityofinglewood.org/about/city_history.asp

granvillenorthdakoka.com History of Egg Creek Township

historicmapworks.com Egg Creek Township, 1910

missamerica.org/our-miss-americas/1940/1941

Books

Bawden, James and Ron Miller. *Conversations with Classic Film Stars: Interviews from Hollywood's Golden Era*. University Press of Kentucky, 2016

Behlmer, Rudy. *Memo from Darryl F. Zanuck: The Golden Years at Twentieth Century-Fox.* Grove Press, 1995

Bogle, Donald. *Toms, Coons, Mulattoes, Mammies, & Bucks: An Interpretive History of Blacks in American Films., 3rd Edition.* Continuum, 1997

Brady, Frank. *Citizen Welles: A Biography of Orson Welles.* Scribner, 1989

Carey, Gary and Joseph L. Mankiewicz. *More About All About Eve.* Random House, 1972

Chierichetti, David. *George Seaton.* Louis B. Mayer/American Film Institute, 1975

Crookes, William and T.A. Malone, George Shadbolt. *British Journal of Photography.* Volume 93, 1946

Current Biography 1951: Jeanne Crain

Current Biography 1954: Cid Ricketts Sumner

Current Biography 1967: David Janssen

Dauth, Brian. *Joseph L. Mankiewicz: Interviews.* University Press of Mississippi, 2008

Drummond, Alexander Magnus. *Plays for the Country Theatre.* New York State College of Agriculture, Cornell University, 1922

Enyeart, James. *Willard Van Dyke: Changing the World Through Photography and Film.* UNM Press, 2008

Fujiwara, Chris. *The World and Its Double: The Life and Work of Otto Preminger.* Farrar, Straus and Giroux, 2015

Gans, Eric Lawrence. *Carole Landis: A Most Beautiful Girl.* University Press of Mississippi, 2008

Garrison, Omar V. *Howard Hughes in Las Vegas.* L. Stuart, 1970

Gussow, Mel. *Darryl F. Zanuck: Don't Say Yes Until I Finish Talking.* Da Capo Press, 1980

Gavin, James. *Stormy Weather: The Life of Lena Horne.* Simon and Schuster, 2009

Geist, Kenneth L. *Pictures Will Talk: The Life and Films of Joseph L. Mankiewicz.* Scribner, 1978

Gladstone, B. James. *The Man Who Seduced Hollywood: The Life and Loves of Greg Bautzer, Tinseltown's Most Powerful Lawyer.* Chicago Review Press, 2013

Goodman, Ezra. *The Fifty-Year Decline and Fall of Hollywood.* Simon and Schuster, 1961

Hannsberry, Karen Burroughs. *Femme Noir: Bad Girls of Film.* McFarland, 1998

Hirsch, Foster. *Otto Preminger: The Man Who Would Be King.* Knopf Doubleday Publishing Group, 2011

Jewel, Richard B. and Vernon Harbin. *The RKO Story.* Arlington House, 1982

Kazan, Elia. *Elia Kazan: A Life.* Anchor Books, Doubleday, 1989

Kotsilibas-Davis, James and Myrna Loy. *Myrna Loy: Being and Becoming.* Alfred A. Knopf, 1987

Leslie, Thomas. *Iowa State Fair: Country Comes to Town.* Princeton Architectural Press, 2007

Lev, Peter. *Twentieth Century-Fox: The Zanuck-Skouras Years, 1935–1965.* University of Texas Press, 2013

McBride, Joseph. *Searching for John Ford: A Life.* Faber & Faber, 2004

McClelland, Doug. *Forties Film Talk: Oral Histories of Hollywood.* McFarland & Company, 1992

McGilligan, Patrick. *George Cukor: A Double Life*. St. Martin's Press, 1991

McKay, James. *Dana Andrews: The Face of Noir*. McFarland, 2010

Mortensen, William and Larry Lytle, A. D. Coleman, Michael Moynihan. *American Grotesque: The Life and Art of William Mortensen*. Feral House, 2014

Mosley, Leonard. *Zanuck: The Rise and Fall of Hollywood's Last Tycoon*. Little, Brown and Company, 1984

Parish, James Robert. *The Fox Girls*. Arlington House, 1971

Phillips, Gene D. *George Cukor*. Twayne Publishers, 1982

Pratley, Gerald. *The Cinema of Otto Preminger*. A. Zwemmer, 1971

Preminger, Otto. *Preminger: An Autobiography*. Doubleday, 1977

Price, Victoria. *Vincent Price: A Daughter's Biography*. Open Road Media, 2014

Rodgers, Richard. *Musical Stages: An Autobiography*. Da Capo Press, 2009

Russell, Jane. *Jane Russell: An Autobiography, My Path & My Detour*. Jove edition, 1986

Schnittkind, Henry T. ed. *The Poets of the Future: A College Anthology for 1920-1921*. Stratford, 1921

Staggs, Sam. *All About All About Eve: The Complete Behind-the-Scenes Story of the Bitchiest Film Ever Made*. St. Martin's Press, 2001

Tierney, Gene and Mickey Herskowitz. *Self-Portrait*. Wyden Books, 1979

Teiser, Ruth and Catherine Harroun. *Conversations with Ansel Adams*, 1972

Torme, Mel. *My Singing Teachers*. Oxford University Press, 1994

Waters, Ethel with Charles Samuels. *His Eye is On the Sparrow: An Autobiography.* Da Capo Press Edition, 1992

Made in the USA
Coppell, TX
28 December 2023

26939200R00142